Native American Herbalism

A Detailed Guide to Ancient Herbs and Their Health Benefits

(Find Out Hundreds of Magic Herbal Remedies and Practice in Real Life the Best Herbalism)

Charles Dodd

Published By **Bengion Cosalas**

Charles Dodd

Native American Herbalism: A Detailed Guide to Ancient Herbs and Their Health Benefits (Find Out Hundreds of Magic Herbal Remedies and Practice in Real Life the Best Herbalism)

ISBN   978-1-7771462-7-6

No part of this guidebook shall be reproduced in any form without permission in writing from the publisher except in the case of brief quotations embodied in critical articles or reviews.

Legal & Disclaimer

The information contained in this book is not designed to replace or take the place of any form of medicine or professional medical advice. The information in this book has been provided for educational & entertainment purposes only.

The information contained in this book has been compiled from sources deemed reliable, and it is accurate to the best of the Author's knowledge; however, the Author cannot guarantee its accuracy and validity and cannot be held liable for any errors or omissions. Changes are periodically made to this book. You must consult your doctor or get professional medical advice before using any of the suggested remedies, techniques, or information in this book.

Table Of Contents

Chapter 1: Native American Herbs

1. Agave

The Binomial name is Agave Americana

Location: Southern United States (mainly in California, Arizona, and Nevada) and Mexico.

The characteristics: A squat central stem that's barely noticeable is the main feature of this perennial plant. The leaves of succulents are tall, pointed and a greenish-grayish hue. When it reaches sexual maturation (it could take as long as 20 years) the plant produces only one flower out of an erect spike. the flower dies.

Parts to be collected for medical use leaves.

The preferred solvent is water or alcohol.

Main effect: Diuretic, Anti-inflammatory.

Native American Use:

* The sap can be extremely sticky and may bond the edges of an open injury for use as an emergency medical.

If taken in a large amount, may cause poisoning. Because of this, natives from in the South Western states used agave leaves to catch fish. They placed the leaves in an pond, or a enclosed area in an area of a river. The poison in them temporarily paralyzed the fish that passed through within the area. As a result, they were able to swim on the surface, and were easy picks.

This juice is utilized to treat inflammation and for diuretic properties.

Modern use:

"Agave Hearts" are famous as a source of making tequila.

It is not widely known that Progesterone hormones commonly prescribed during pregnancies to support proper growth of the fetus are extracted from the Agave leaf.

Additionally, the roots are often utilized in the creation of soaps that are natural because of their rich content of saponins. This means you are able to make excellent natural shampoo and soap by making juice by grating and by squeezing the agave roots.

In the end the Agave nectar has been employed as a substitute for sugar because of its low impact on the body, and also decreasing the stop-effect of fat burning which sweet ingredients can have on your body.

Alder

Binomial Name: Alnus rubra

Area: All wet and humid areas in Canada and the United States and Canada.

Specifications: Alders are trees with a medium-sized size (about 70 feet high). The bark covering the trunk is amorphous appearance based on the time of the tree's age. It may appear smooth and gray in an infant tree or coarse and light-colored for an old one. The leaves are oval with a pointed end with serrated edges. The flowers are catkins with various sizes based on gender of the flower: male yellow-green flowers are large and extend downwards; females have smaller and the red cones are. These, in turn, produce in the event of pollination, cones containing flat seeds.

Parts that can be collected for medical use The most common is bark.

The preferred solvent is water.

Main effect: Astringent, Cathartic, Tonic.

Native American Use:

The female ament decoction is utilized to treat sexual transmitted Disorders like Gonorrhea.

* The poultice of male flowers was consumed to increase stool movement in cases of constipation.

Poultices made of fresh leaves were utilized to heal cuts and skin irritations, and the ash resulting from the combustion of leaves was utilized as toothpaste.

* Tea made from dried leaves provides the ability to reduce inflammation if you use it to cleanse the area of skin when there is a urticarial skin rash.

* The decoctions of boiling barks possess the effect of astringent as well as febrifuge. It is also being used today to soothe sore throat. Utilize fresh inner bark for maximum effect.

Aloe Vera

A binomial name: Aloe vera

Area A: The Southern United States, especially Southeastern ones.

The characteristic of the plant is that at the base of the plant is a rosette at the base consisting of pointed, long succulent leaves, with edges that are toothed. Its color is olive green. occasionally flecked with yellow. It forms a cluster of yellow or red tubular flowers that grow from a central flower spike.

Parts that can be collected for use in medical research: Leaves juice.

The preferred solvent is water.

The main effect is: Tonic, Emmenagogue, Vermifuge, Cathartic, Depurative

Native American Use:

Poultice made of fresh leaves could be used for treating wounds, burns, and insect bites all over the world. One of the most obscurities with the poultice of fresh leaves is the fact that it was placed in cheesecloth, which was then dried. The poultice that dried was milled to produce an extremely fine powder which was applied as a application to open wounds in order to stop bleeding, and also for blisters to soak up fluid and prevent infection. In the event of diluting it into water the powder could be used for menstrual control or for the elimination of intestinal parasites.

Warning: Do not use during pregnancy the gallbladder or liver condition or hemorrhoids.

Amaranth

Binomial Name: Amaranthus retrolexus

The location is diffused all throughout all over the United States and Canada in meadows and prairies.

Specifications: This plant stands about 4 feet and features oval-shaped, gray-green rough leaves. In the flower's interior, in the fall, you will find a variety of smaller black seeds. The taproots are of red.

Parts to be collected to treat medical conditions: Leaves and flowers.

The preferred solvent is water.

Main effect: Astringent.

Native American Use:

* The raw or decoction consumption of leaves was utilized to treat astringent symptoms as well as to decrease excessive menstrual flow (hypermenorrhea). The decoction made of leaves was also utilized as a gargle to treat throat irritation.

* Seeds were used to make an energy source for the long-term. They can be ground and used to make cakes or bread. Leafs (raw as well as cooked) as well as roots (boiled) are also edible.

Angelica

Binomial Name: Angelica atropurpurea

The location is Wet Lowlands in the North-Eastern States.

Specifications: 6 feet tall with thick purple stems. The leaves are big and split into three to five smaller oval-shaped leaves, which are smaller. They are organized into umbels. They are tinier and white. They are very identical to the hemlock however, this is poisonous. To make sure you can identify it The best way to determine the species is to smell the root or seeds. If they have that typical angelica smell that is comparable to celery, then they are angelica. Another way to double-check is to cut branches or leaves and sniff. If the smell is similar to urine, it's Hemlock.

The parts to be collected to use for medical reasons: roots flowers, leaves.

The preferred solvent is boiling water.

Main effect: Carminative, expectorant, diuretic, emmenagogue.

Native American Use:

*The application of fresh root poultice to swollen joints, or on any concussion from minor to serious resulted in an anti-inflammatory as well as pain relief effect for the area being treated.

* This decoction was the most preferred method for Natives to get the phytochemicals as well as to make Angelica for health purposes.

In more details, the concoction of flowers and leaves was utilized to treat all kinds of ailments: arthritis, fevers, sore throats ulcers Urinary Tract Infections, as well as headaches. The decoction was believed to be a cure to treat all ailments.

It's an effective carminative that assists with gastric digestion. It is also a potent anti-inflammatory gargle to use in the case of a sore throat.

* Raw consumption of leaves was valued for its characteristic of being astringent to help treat diarrhea. This same effect is explained as a result of the intake of root.

The use of decoctions from seeds was to reduce menstrual flow when there was hypermenorrhea.

According to me, the most effective method for Angelica belief is through tinctures. The tincture of roots (dosage 40 drops 3-4 times per every day) as well as seeds (dosage 20 drops 3-4 times per daily) can be beneficial for treating the above mentioned condition with a speedy manner.

* Other applications of Angelica in Native American culture, besides its medicinal purpose and the connection to religious beliefs (dried leaves as well as flowers were utilized for smoking during the ceremony of the sacred pipe).

Chapter 2: Balsam Fir

Binomial Name: Abies balsamea

Locality: North of the United States or South of Canada within forests.

Specifications: Evergreen trees with a height of up to 65 feet. tall. The gray bark often leaks sap, and its appearance changes according to its age. tree Smooth for young trees, coarser for more mature ones. The leaves are needle-green at the top while the lower part is white. Cones are about 4 inches long as well as red/purple.

The parts to be collected to use for medical reasons These include: roots, sap, leaves and barks.

The preferred solvent is boiling water.

The main effect is analgesic and antiseptic.

Native American Use:

* The bark decoction were used to decrease the fever and to stimulate sweating in order in order to flush the body of toxins.

Additionally, the tea was employed to treat respiratory issues and colds because of its astringent qualities.

The sap is directly used to treat burns as well as close wounds. The raw consumption of the sap can help prevent sore throats and colds.

The only use for the balsamic sap occurred during the sweat lodge ceremony. The sap was sprinkled onto hot stones in order to produce fragrant steam.

Balsam Root

Binomial Name: Balsamorhiza sagittaria

Location: Foothills of Rocky Mountains.

The characteristics of the plant are small (one up to 2 feet in height). The leaves are hairy and arrow-shaped to the touch. They tend to be found in the lower portion in the plant (basal). The flowers are bright yellow in the petals as well as on the stamens. The flowers are protruding with a protruding.

Parts that are to be collected to use for medical reasons This includes the entire plant.

The preferred solvent is boiling water.

The main effect is antibacterial as well as antiseptic.

Native American Use:

* Consuming raw leaves improves the immune system and is regarded as a preventive treatment for flu and colds. The leaves poultice is great for treating burns and wounds. It can serve as dressing wounds when you've hurt yourself on the wood. When you chew some leaves before placing the poultice over the wound, you'll reap all the benefits of saliva as well as the balsamroot.

For more serious injury, it's possible to apply the adhesive sap to join the edges of the wounded.

* The mixture of roots and leaves was utilized to treat stomachaches, colds and other

symptoms associated with sexually transmitted diseases like sensation of burning due to gonorrhea.

• As a food item The plant is eaten raw, in all of its components, however the roots can be bitter. Cooking them can remove bitterness.

Barberry

Binomial Name: Berberis canadensis

The location: It is found in the forests of all Northern United States and in Canada in general. Canada.

The characteristics of this shrub are that it is thorny along its branches. They it can reach at least 8 feet high. Leaves grow in groupings on the branches. They're succulent and simple with teeth at their ends. Large clusters of bright yellow blooms line the ends of branches. They have six sepals, and transform into scarlet Ovoid fruit after pollination.

Parts that should be collected for medical use such as barks, berries, leaves.

The preferred solvent is alcohol, water.

Main effect: Antiseptic, carminative, febrifuge.

Native American Use:

* The decoction derived from the bark can be considered as a remedy to treat diarrhea and also to treat throat sores. The bark was also applied as a topically treatment by cutting it down to poultice and putting directly to mouth ulcers as well as injuries. It helped to heal the area due to its antiseptic qualities.

* Fruits were utilized as food (WARNING drinking too much can result in diarrhea) as well as for health reasons: decoctions of berries was utilized to treat fevers in cases where other treatments failed.

The decoction of leaves was believed to be beneficial in detoxifying the liver.

* Lastly, the roots were utilized for medicinal reasons, both cooked and raw Poultices of the fresh root was used to stimulate saliva and

increase the appetite of those recuperating from illness and their juice was utilized as a cleanser for burns, wounds and scratches due to its antiseptic effects.

Bearberry

Binomial Name: Arctostaphylos uva ursi

Area: All across Northern as well as Western United States and in the entirety of Canada In the forests.

The characteristics of this low-lying evergreen dwarf tree is a cover for the forest. Leaves are oval, smooth and large. The calyx is shaped in spring and small white-pinkish blooms appear in tiny groups on the upper part of stems. They are round drupes, with typically three seeds that are hard inside.

Parts that are collected to use for medical purposes Leaves.

Most preferred solvents are alcohol and water.

Main effect: Diuretic, astringent.

Native American Use:

* The leaves of Bearberry were extensively utilized by Native Americans to treat ailments and for ceremonial reasons. It was a plant of sacred significance that was used in each crucial Native American ceremony, especially during the sacred pipe ritual.

* Lakota used to call it chaNGsasa Ojibwe asemaa Menominee Ahpaesawan. However, the name that gained popularity to Europeans to describe it refers to the Unami Delaware term for "mixture", Kinnikinnick.

In addition to the traditional usage of the plant, the medical uses are numerous that range from the use of poultices made from leaves to reduce bleeding from wounds because of its astringent properties to decoctions of berries and leaves that is used to treat bladder or kidney disorders or to treat mild pain.

* Additionally the salve made from the leaves was applied to sores and rashes: the Leaves

were cooked extremely low temperatures in animal fat for 1 day. In order to achieve the proper size, beeswax was added to the melting fat.

An easy preparation that which you can make at the ease in your kitchen, to reap the benefits of this plant's incredible properties is Phytochemicals Alcoholic Extract. Simply soaking the leaves for one week in a mason bottle protected from sunlight, you will be able to obtain the most potent analgesic to treat headaches. The suggested dosage is one teaspoon of the alcohol extraction in one cup of water, two every daily.

Finally, Natives used Bearberry for meals dried Kinnikinnick the berries were crushed in order to make a powder that was utilized as a spice as well, fresh berries were cooked before being cooked in animal fat until they were soft enough for mash.

ADVICE: Avoid using during pregnancy.

Chapter 3: Beech

Binomial Name: Fagus grandifolia

Location: The Eastern United States and Southeast of Canada. It is a favorite in sun-lit environments.

The characteristics of this beautiful high tree could be up to 120 feet tall. The trunk's central part is covered with smooth gray bark. It has large, dense branches that are surrounded with many leaves. They are deep veined, oval-shaped, with teethed edges. Leaves drop in the autumn like all deciduous trees. The fruits are tiny four-lobed nuts that are covered in soft red thorn hair.

Parts that are collected to treat medical conditions such as leaves, bark.

Most preferred solvent: water.

Main effect: Antibacterial, Astringent.

Native American Use:

* The decoction made of beech leaves and barks helps in treating diarrhea and dysentery

due to its astringent properties. The decoction also was used to treat liver ailments (also the modern medical profession uses it for treating diabetes) and bladder problems. The dosage and method recommended for this remedy is 1 tsp dried leaves or bark per every cups of water that is boiling drinking three tablespoons in the morning before eating your main meal.

Black Cohosh

Binomial Name: Actaea racemosa

The location includes meadows, forests and prairies that are found in Canada's Northern United States and Southern Canada.

The characteristics of this evergreen plant is fashioned from a rhizome that's black and green with a straight, green stem, which is about six feet in its prime. The leaves are broad, basal and organized into compounds composed of three leaflets, each with teethed margins. The flowers are clustered within racemes that are densely populated and are characterized by an erect stigma that is surrounded by stamens protruding outward, but without a petals or sepals.

Parts that are needed for medical use Parts to collect for medical purposes: Root.

The preferred solvent is boiling water.

Main effect: Diuretic, diaphoretic, expectorant, sedative, emmenagogue.

Native American Use:

* Black Cohosh root decoction was extensively utilized by Natives for treating coughs and also as a blood purifier. A different application was for the treatment for hypo-menorrhoida (poor menstrual flow) as well as to cause abortions.

An easy preparation of the black cohosh that you will be able to do in a matter of minutes is to make the alcoholic infusion. The preparation has proven to be extremely successful for curing Rheumatism. Instructions for making the remedy are simple to follow simply soak freshly harvested black cohosh root in alcohol, with an approximate weight ratio of 1:8 over a period of one week. The suggested dosage for the hypothesis is one teaspoon of the alcohol extract in a cup of water, twice each daily.

WARNING: Do not use during pregnancy.

Black Gum

Binomial Name: Nyssa sylvatica

The location stretches from the Eastern Coast to the United States to East Texas with wet conditions.

Specifications: This tree is able to grow up to 80 feet in height. The broad central trunk is coated with scaled and deep-indented brown-red bark. Numerous branches with brown-reddish leaves emerge of the trunk and can be seen in any direction. They have alternate leaves and are lance-shaped with sleek edges. The flowers in yellow are female and male. They grow in circular clusters, arranged on pedicels.

The parts to be collected to treat medical conditions: bark and root.

Most preferred solvent: Boiling water.

Main effect: Diuretic, diaphoretic, expectorant, sedative, emmenagogue.

Native American Use:

* The decoction derived from black gum bark could assist in the treatment of mild respiratory problems. The bark decoction also worked in the form of a bath when a childbirth was difficult.

* Lastly, the "jelly juice" of the root was utilized as an eye wash.

Black Haw

Binomial Name: Viburnum prunifolium

The location is diffused all across North America (the United States as well as Canada) but mostly within the east cost zone.

Specifications: On average this tree is able to attain 20 feet. in size. It is gray with a brown outer bark, and deep green toothed oval leaves. Roots have a brown-reddish hue and the flowers are with white clumps. The fruits are dark blackberries that have flavor that is sweet.

Parts that should be gathered to use for medical reasons: bark and the root bark.

Most preferred solvents are water and alcohol.

Main effect: Diuretic, astringent, nervine, antispasmodic.

Native American Use:

* Native American healers used Black Haw root bark to stop miscarriages among women that had an increased risk of it due to the previous experience or experiencing indications of uterus contractions. The treatment was to drink the decoction of root bark 3 weeks prior to of the miscarriage that occurred and for a period of three weeks following. If there was no miscarriage from another uterus contraction occurred after

three weeks of treatment, it is possible to stop the remedy.

* The advantages of the decoction made of root bark didn't limit the prevention of miscarriages. In fact, it's well-known for its effectiveness to treat febrifugrees effectively as well as in cases of diarrhea, when all other treatment options failed.

Additionally, it can have positive effects on heart beat problems, menstrual issues and cramps.

Bloodroot

Binomial Name: Sanguinaria canadensis

The location is scattered across the eastern portion of North America. Starting from the Eastern coastline of Canada within the North up to north to the Great Lakes region, down to the Mississippi River in the South.

Specifications: This tiny low-lying species can grow to the height of 7 inches. size. Its stem grows from a twisting, red Rhizome, which releases a red sap when squeezed (hence the term) and usually has up to five leaves. They are greenish-grayish with several leaves (five up to 7). It is white, with 10 to 12 petals as well as the central stamens are yellow.

The parts to be collected for medical use Parts to collect for medical purposes: Root.

The preferred solvent is water, alcohol.

Main effect: Antibacterial, expectorant, sedative, emetic.

Native American Use:

* The Bloodroot plant was known to indigenous people as a potent medication and could cause vomiting if consumed in large amounts. The use of bloodroot was in the event for food poisoning.

A different use of this root is for the topical use of the juice in treating warts.

The extraction double of the root is utilized in moderate amounts for treating respiratory ailments ranging from mild to extreme, like laryngitis, cough, asthma.

* The extract of the root that is alcoholic has sanguinarine in it, and is used in the present for topically treated treatment of skin cancer.

Another use for the root extract is to act in repelling mosquitos and other insects. The Native Americans applied the extract on their bodies in order to protect themselves from insects from biting them. That's the reason Native Americans were called red skins when they first met Europeans.

Blueberry

Binomial Name: Vaccinium

Locality: All over North Unites States as well as Canada In forests and plains.

Specifications: This group of plants is close to the ground in the majority of the species. The height of different varieties of this plant can differ greatly, ranging from a couple of inches to 15 feet. The leaves of the branches of wood are in a series and are oval. The flowers are pinkish white and bell-shaped. They form groups that are at the top on the branches. The fruit is round, dark blue if ripe, and sweet.

Parts that can be collected to use for medical reasons: leaves and fruits.

Most preferred solvents: Boiling water or alcohol.

Main effect: Diuretic, astringent.

Native American Use:

* Native Americans prepared tea using dried leaves to use as a treatment for diarrhea. made use of this tea to treat dermatologic conditions such as dermatitis and itching of every kind.

A fascinating application for this tree was that it is used to drink of of dried leaves, which immediately lessens the nausea sensation.

In relation to the fruits aside from the obvious consumption raw one of the most simple recipes which you could make from the comfort of your home can be the infusion of alcohol for treating spasmodic diarrhea as well as IBS. The steps are simple to follow: put dried blueberries in an open bottle in glass and then over the bottle with a mixture of 95 percent alcohol. The suggested dosage to use this method is 1 tablespoon. of the infusion containing alcohol in 4 oz. of distillated water.

Chapter 4: Blue False Indigo

Binomial Name: Baptisia australis

Dispersed all over the Eastern up to Midwestern United States, at the woods' edges and within meadows.

Specifications: This perennial can reach at least 5 feet. The green, pale stem rises directly from the rhizome's central part that is surrounded by alternate leaves comprised of three oval leaflets. The flowers bloom in June and form races. They look like peas and have a blue/purple color. They resemble peapods that have been inflated. more sharper edges and the seeds of a pod that are yellow.

Parts to be collected to use for medical reasons The Roots.

Most preferred solvent: water.

Main effect: Emetic, purgative, astringent.

Native American Use:

* The natives utilized the tea made from the plant's roots to help treat diarrhea, nausea

and toothache. They also used it to wash the skin to treat conjunctivitis.

Contrarily eating raw the plant may cause vomiting and nausea because of the mild toxic effects.

ADVICE: Avoid consumption when you are pregnant or nursing.

Boneset

Binomial Name: Epatorium perfoliatum

Area: All across Canada and the Eastern United States and Canada and Canada, especially in humid environments.

The characteristics of this perennial plant are that it is able to grow as tall as 5 feet. The stems that rise from the ground are adorned with opposite tall, pointed, long leaves, with margins that are toothed. The stem cuts through one huge broad leaf. The pink-white flowers appear in a cluster near the top of stems.

Parts to be collected to use for medical reasons: leaves and flowers.

The preferred solvent is water, alcohol.

Main effect: Febrifuge, diaphoretic, carminative.

Native American Use:

* Native Americans used boneset leaves and other flowers to make many medicinal remedies. In particular, the tea derived from infusions from dried leaf was thought to be an effective febrifuge. It was used as a treatment of the most serious diseases including pneumonia, malaria as well as arthritis and gout.

In discussing gout as well as arthritis, it's important to discuss the application to the skin of the poultice that is made from pounding of flowers and fresh leaves to provide a application of a topical anti-inflammatory on swelling joints, as well as any other injuries on joints.

* The infusion double of roots was utilized to alleviate the symptoms of food poisoning as well as to treat sore throats with gargling.

ADVICE: If taken in large amounts the drug could cause vomiting and liver damage.

Buckthorn (Cascara Sagrada)

Benomial Name Rhamnus purshiana or cathartica

Locality: R. Cathartica can be located along Lake Michigan shores while R. Purshiana is found throughout the North-West region of the North-American continent.

The characteristics of these shrubs are compact and packed with leaves and berries. The branches are gray brown bark, with white lenticels. have slim, oval-shaped and white, green leaves. Flowers are white, small with a rounded shape, they are placed in large bunches. Fruits are round and orange/yellow as they mature. They have three seeds in the middle.

Items to gather to use for medical reasons: bark and roots.

The preferred solvent is boiling water or alcohol.

Main effect: Purgative, emetic, vermifuge.

Native American Use:

* Ojibway was utilized to make the infusion of buckthorn bark to increase bowel movements and eliminate intestinal worms. This plant is known for its mild toxicity and decoctions of the young fruit and branches was utilized to treat food poisoning.

* Native Americans' protocol to gather the barks was in accordance with the natural cycles of this plant. The bark was collected between the beginning of spring until the start of summer. This is when the bark becomes soft and less difficult to take off. They dried the bark for at least a year in a cool, shaded location to keep it in good condition and increase the healing qualities.

NOTE: The bark decoction is not to be used in any way to treat an intestinal obstruction. Furthermore, continual consumption is not recommended due to the fact that Buckthorn can be carcinogenic when used regularly.

California Poppy

Binomial Name: Eschscholzia californica

The location is Western Coast of the United States as well as Canada Dry environments.

Specifications: A small flowering plant with a height of 30 inches typically. Leaf leaves are not numerous, broken into a number of small blue-green leaflets and pointed ones. One flower which emerges from the soil has four vibrant yellow-orange petals. The seeds of small black are inside the flower.

Parts that are to be collected to use for medical reasons This includes the entire plant.

The preferred solvent is water, alcohol.

Principal effect: Sedative diuretic and analgesic.

Native American Use:

* As with all poppy varieties, the California poppy is famous for its effects on sedation. Native Americans used to give tea made from dried leaves and flowers in order to lessen anxiety and ease anxious attacks. It was also known to ease menstrual discomfort as well as facilitating diuresis. Additionally, the tea is poisonous to bugs and other parasites, and is employed as a shampoo for head lice.

* The sap as with all poppies are where the substances that induce sedation are the most than the rest. The indigenous people were aware of this and would apply directly to gums in order for pain relief.

* Native Americans also used to chew on the roots in order to absorb this sap, which is sedative. It was used to treat toothaches and headaches.

A nebulous use for this plant is the seedpods and their sticky resin upon removal out of the plant. The resin encourages lactation when it is smudged on Nipples.

ADVICE: Avoid when pregnant.

Catnip

Binomial Name: Nepeta cataria

The location is diffused all across North America

The characteristics of this perennial with many branches, can reach four feet in height. Leaves are small, oval and grey-white, with slender edges. Lilac-colored flowers are small. They are borne from the top of the stem, in huge groups.

Parts to be collected to use for medical reasons: leaves or stems and even flowers.

The preferred solvent is boiling alcohol, water.

Main effect: Carminative, tonic, diaphoretic, emmenagogue.

Native American Use:

* Native Americans used the infusion of the entire plant (leaves along with stems, leaves, as well as flowers) to help with intestinal disorders. The tonic effects is a great way to reduce the spasms in the intestinal tract and eases the inflammation that is associated with dysentery and diarrhea. This infusion also is carminative which aids in treating intestinal gas. The infusion was specifically recommended for menstrual cramps that were achy and dysmenorrhea.

* A different use for the tea was due to its diaphoretic nature: the increased sweating could aid reduce fever and also in helping to promote general detoxification in the body.

A different use for the plant was for the top-of-the-line application of the poultice made from catnip on joints with swelling to ease pain and inflammation in cases of gout or arthritis.

WARNING: Do not use during pregnancy.

Cattail

Binomial Name: Typha latifolia or Typha angustifolia

Where: Cattail can be found throughout North America, in wet habitats (lakeshores streams, bogs, lakes ...)

Specifications: A long spear-shaped plants that can reach 8 feet high. It blooms two times in the spring season that look like hot dogs on sticks. The larger one, situated within the lower portion of the plant is female while the other one, located in the top part of the plant, is the male one, that disappears following the dispersal of the pollen.

The parts to be collected to use for medical reasons: roots and leaves.

The preferred solvent is boiling water.

Main effect: Anodyne, emollient.

Native American Use:

* Native Americans widely used the mix of roots for an application for sunburn treatments due to its emollient qualities.

Additionally, the flowers were utilized to treat wounds since they stop bleeding and suck up excess water. Additionally, the ashes produced from burning leaves have antiseptic properties and could be used to seal burns and wounds.

Apart from the therapeutic use of the plant, indigenous people consumed it for their food. specifically, the roots were dried, then ground to produce flour for porridge and bread, while heart meat was cooked and consumed as a vegetable.

Chamomile

Binomial Name: Matricaria matricarioides

The location is diffused all across North America

Specifications: A small flower with up to 20 inches tall in the wild, which tends to grow along the path. It has yellow pollen as well as a white corolla petals. The leaves are bright green and long, and have small laciniae.

Parts that should be collected for use in medicine: Flowers and herbs.

Most preferred solvents are water and alcohol.

Principal effect: Nervine an antispasmodic and sedative.

Native American Use:

* The dried or fresh plant extract was utilized to alleviate stomach pains and relieve excess intestinal gas. In addition, the infusion also had a positive effect in treating dysmenorrhea, menstrual cramps and menstrual cramps or, if it was placed on top of the skin, it helped reduce skin irritations such as acne and eczema.

* It was employed as a calming agent for nerves as well as to reduce anxiety and anxiety attacks. Its mild sedative effects is also utilized to treat arthritis and painful joints swelling.

The most well-known application for this amazing herb has to do with preservation of meat. The dried herb, powdered and dried, was used applied to meats to help take in moisture and keep it from turning rotting.

AVOID: Chamomile can trigger reactions that are allergic.

Chapter 5: Corn

Binomial Name: Zea mays

Dispersed throughout the North-Eastern as well as the Central United States and in the entire Central as well as the South American continent.

Specifications: Corn belongs to the Poaceae family. It's six to nine foot long spear-shaped flower that has two kinds of flowers. Female flowers are lower and are also known as corncobs. The ones that are on the at the top are male.

The parts to be collected for use in medicine For example: green pistils, cornsilk.

Most preferred solvent is Diluted Alcohol.

Main effect: Diuretic, emollient.

Native American Use:

Apart from its well-known use in food production it was also utilized for medical purposes.

* An additional use of young silk in relation to the tincture. It was made by maceration process of freshly minced silk in a 50 percent alcohol solution. The suggested weight ratio between the herb and the 50 percent alcohol solution is 1:1 The recommended time for soaking is two weeks at an area that is shaded.

* The tincture contains twenty drops combined with twenty drops Damiana tincture, following the main meal, is the best remedy against Urinary tract infection.

Cranberry

Binomial Name: Vaccinium oxycoccus

The location is North in the US In wet areas

Specifications: This tiny, evergreen plant can be found in the middle of the forest's ground. The woody branches feature the smooth and black bark. Flowers tend to be single and are located near the top of branches. They're white and pinkish, with a bell-like shape with the petals curled upwards. The fruit is round and red.

Parts that should be collected to use for medical reasons such as fruits, bark.

The preferred solvent is water, dilute alcohol.

Main effect: Diuretic, astringent, tonic.

Native American Use:

* Natives utilized the medicinal benefits of cranberries for the treatments for Urinary Tissue Infections. The use of cranberries is in practice today in cases of kidney stones and cystitis.

* In order to absolve their original reason, the berries could be consumed as raw or juiced or, in the case of only available dried or tea form, they were consumed as tea. They are scientifically proved to reduce the pH in the urine, thereby promoting the dissolution of renal stones. They also reduce the growth of the bacterial infections that can cause UTIs.

*The tea made using barks, instead of dried berries was highly efficient in relieving menstrual discomfort and dysmenorrhea. Additionally, it was employed as a skin wash for wounds infected with infection and wounds, because of its astringent qualities it aided in the development of scarred tissues.

Damiana

Binomial Name: Turnera diffusa

Distribution: widely distributed throughout Texas as well as throughout the rest area of Central America.

The characteristics of this small plant may grow up to three feet in height. The halo of branches rises from the ground and bears several lance-shaped, slender leaves that are edge serrated. Flowers with five petals in yellow, as well as five stamens of yellow come at the top of branches.

Parts to be collected for medical use leaves.

Most preferred solvent: water or dilute alcohol.

The main effect is antiseptic and antifungal. stimulant, diuretic.

Native American Use:

* Native Americans used dried leaves in the preparation of a tea for treating Urinary Tract Infections, as well as bladder problems in general. In addition to this it was known as an aphrodisiac of repute and was believed to boost sexual endurance for females as well as males.

* Damiana was also a sacred plant, and was believed to cause hallucinations when taken in large amounts. Native Americans said that it permitted spirits to talk with healers through hallucinations.

Warning: Avoid using during pregnancy or lactation concerns. The recommended dosage in every situation can be as high as 10 grams of dried leaves daily.

Dandelion

A Binomial Name: Taraxacum Officinale

Dispersed all across the south-eastern U.S.

Specifications The most notable characteristic is that in Europe the plant is called "lion tooth". This plant is perennial and can reach as high as 20 inches in the height. It has a taproot and a crown with the basal large, green with deeply toothed leaves. The branches that grow from the base leaves are green and straight, carrying flowers over. They are yellow, round and have a large number of flowers. Every flower is a hermaphrodite meaning it has both female and male features. When the flower heads are pollinated, transforms into spherical clusters, referred to as blow balls. In them, seeds are clustered. They can be dry, and they are umbrella-shaped, allowing them to be easily pushed around by the wind.

Parts that are collected to use for medical reasons The Roots.

Most preferred solvent: water or Alcohol diluted.

Main effect: Diuretic, deobstruent, tonic.

Native American Use:

In addition to the intake of leaves as meals, Native Americans used dandelion as well for its medicinal qualities.

In reality, roots were utilized for detoxification and cleansing for gallbladder or liver problems because it aided digestion and also had an effect of laxative. The diuretic properties of this decoction was widely recognized as well as the antispasmodic effects of the dandelion could also be employed to treat menstrual cramps as well as premenstrual Syndrome.

* Root decoction was employed to improve lactation as well as increase appetite through increasing the production of bile.

It is established scientifically proven that dandelion consumption reduces cholesterol levels in blood circulation. It is because of the fact that it decreases the absorption of cholesterol from foods.

Devil's Club

Name of the Binomial: Oplopanax horridus

Place This is the North-Western States, in wet or shaded conditions

Specifications: This bushy tree is an incredibly close relative of the ginseng. The stems in the central and lesser ones are filled with sharp thorns. Leaves are spiral-shaped and emerge from the stems. They have many lobes and hairy poduncles. White flowers that are small are set in umbels that are spherical on the top in the stem. The fruit is bright red Drupes.

The parts to be collected to use for medical reasons: root and barks.

The preferred solvent is boiling alcohol, water.

Main effect: Tonic.

Native American Use:

* The Native Americans used this plant for ritual and religious motives. The root bark extract was often used as a tonic for nerves, due to the similarity of ginseng to it. In addition it was also used as a dye to treat tissues as well as for a classic body painting technique for warriors (ashes of the devil's club were incorporated into grease in order to make the painting which was believed to shield from combat).

Douglas Maple

The Binomial Name is Acer glabrum.

Distribution: Mostly distributed across areas such as the North-West part of Canada, the United States and Western Canada.

Particulars: This tree could reach 35 feet high. The leaves are broad, trilobed with pointed edges with serrated margins. They are divided into corymbs of 10 and are yellow in hue. The seeds have vertical "leaflets" such as a helicopter. They can travel long distances once they break off to the trees.

Parts that can be collected to treat medical conditions: Leaves and barks.

The preferred solvent is water.

Main effect: Astringent, anti-Inflammatory.

Native American Use:

* Native Americans used the tea made from dried barks and leaves to ease fevers and to treat diarrhea and dysentery. It was treatment for all sorts of illnesses when treatment options weren't available. Poultice made from fresh leaves was utilized to treat joint swelling and to treat rheumatism.

Echinacea/ American Coneflower

Binomial Name: Echinacea purpurea

The area is spread across plains of Central and Eastern United States. Eastern as well as the Central United States.

The characteristics of this plant are composed of a single stem which is three feet tall. The flower itself is of purple, and has an umbrella shape. The stem is covered in dense pelts of small thorns. The leaves are big as well as rough. Roots appear in the middle of yellow along with dark spots.

The parts to be collected to treat medical conditions: flowers leaves, roots, and leaves.

The preferred solvent is alcohol.

The main effect is febrifuge, sialagogues, diaphoretic, analgesic.

Native American Use:

* The medicinal benefits of Echinacea are well-known all across the globe. In the past, Greeks as well as Egyptians utilized this herb from the beginning of time to treat every illness. Furthermore, Native Americans were aware of the power of this plant and utilized it for treating a myriad of conditions.

* Root decoctions were used to treat sore throats, toothaches, as well as stomach discomfort. Diaphoretic characteristics of Echinacea could be used to stimulate sweating, which helps cleanse the body, and reducing the fever.

The poultice that is made from pounding the leaves and flowers can be used to treat cuts as well as acne and other skin issues. Additionally, eating fresh leaves aids in combating fungal and microbial diseases (such like candida) which has been proved as a potent antiviral.

ADVICE: Consuming Echinacea is not advised when pregnant.

Chapter 6: Evening Primrose

Binomial Name: Oenothera biennis

Place: Found throughout fields and gardens throughout Canada and the United States and Canada.

The characteristics of this small plant is able to sustain a 2 year existence. In the beginning, the flowers aren't visible, but the plant only has the base of a leaf cluster. The second year is when it emerges from ground and is three feet high at the maximum, with serrated Oblong leaves as well as an oblong flower that is crowned. Flowers of yellow open in the evening, and contain four petals with the stamens are protruding in yellow. Seeds are black brown and drop-shaped.

Parts that are collected for medical use Parts to collect for medical purposes: Roots.

The preferred solvent is water.

Native American Use:

* The use for medical purposes of the evening primrose comprises most of it being pounded on the entire plant or portions of it in order to create an ointment.

The poultice made from this plant was utilized in the past by Native Americans to treat wounds as well as burns by applying topical solutions. The poultice made consisting of only the roots was heated prior to application topically to treat hemorrhoids as well as fissures.

A largely unexplored use for this plant's use in herbalism today can be the capacity to lower cholesterol levels through the seeds extract. Simply add the pounded seeds inside a dark and non-metallic container that has an airtight lid covered by a 50% alcohol and water solution. The approximate weight ratio is 1:8, it is important to make adjustments based to the amount that is effective to fill the seeds. The container is then left in the refrigerator for 2 weeks.

Feverfew

Parthenium is a Binomial Name.

The location: It is scattered throughout all over the United States and southern Canada through meadows and gardens.

The characteristics of this tiny flower could grow to 20 inches when in its natural state. It's a simple species with a flower that has the yellow-colored pollen as well as a corolla that is white with petals. Leaves are yellowish greenish and pinnate.

Parts that should be collected to use for medical reasons: flower and herbs.

Most preferred solvents are water and alcohol.

The main effect is nerveine. antispasmodic, sedative and carminative.

Native American Use:

According to the title, Natives used this plant for its ability to reduce fever. Tea derived from this flower can be a potent febrifuge, and it was also utilized for headache relief due to the mild sedative effect.

Geranium

Binomial Name: Geranium

The location is diffused all across all over the Eastern United States.

Specifications: This plant has multiple branches, each with a single flower coming from a central root, and reaching the maximum height is 2 feet. The leaves are typically palmate, with seven lobes each one having edge serrated (depends upon the particular species). Flowers are characterized by five broad petals with different colors ranging according to the species. red, purple, pink and white.

Parts that must be gathered to treat medical conditions: Leaves or flowers and the roots.

The preferred solvent is water.

Main effect: Astringent, Anti-hemorrhagic.

Native American Use:

An under-appreciated usage of geranium is among of the medications used in emergency cases of injuries. It is actually an extremely effective anti-hemorrhagic, and the entire plant (leaves as well as flowers as well as the roots) was crushed in a poultices directly over deep wounds to stop bleeding. The plant is usually chewed in order to make the poultice, and also to contribute to the anti-hemorrhagic and astringent actions, and the antiseptic effect of saliva.

* Root was utilized in poultice as well as decoction: the poultice was then used to treat hemorrhoids. root decoctions were used to treat toothache.

Ginseng

Binomial Name: Panax ginseng

It is located in the south-eastern portion of Canada as well as in the Eastern Part of the United States up to Mississippi. It requires a dry and well-shaded habitat, like huge forests with a huge trees with a large canopy.

Specifications: This tiny perennial is found in shaded, well-drained regions. The basal rhizome is one stem may reach as high as 20 inches size. It's divided into three leaves that are arranged in groups of. Each leaf is comprised of five leaflets that are that are lance-shaped, with crisply sharp edges. The topmost point of the single stem it is an assemblage of small, yellow/green blooms which develop into a cluster of round, bright red seeds.

Parts that should be collected for use in medical research For medical purposes: Roots, particularly dried.

Most preferred solvent is Water.

Main effect: Emollient, nervine, stimulant, febrifuge.

Native American Use:

* The use for ritual purposes of ginseng is well reported by Native Americans. The plant was utilized for its sacred properties to ward off evil spirits away from some of the most sacred events including that of the Green Corn Dance and funerary ones.

* The medicinal usage of this plant is mostly based on its febrifuge effects from the decoction made of the roots that have been dried. It was also believed to be a cleanser in the body, due to its diaphoretic qualities (induce sweating).

The mixture had an antistress and nerve-stress effect. It also slowed the neuromuscular system, and it was utilized in the treatment of injuries (Nervine).

Warning: Excessive consumption (more than 3g daily) could cause dysentery and sleepiness. Avoid while pregnant and lactating.

Warn: Because American wild Ginseng is declining in its numbers as a result, it's considered to be as a threatened species. The one that is grown in China can be used as a alternative, but remember to thoroughly wash it as it's spray-soaked with a fungicide in order to keep its freshness during the travel.

Goldenrod

Binomial Name: Solidago canadensis

The location is scattered across all over the North American continent, from coast to coast, in meadows as well as on the edges of fields that are cultivated.

The characteristics of this perennial plant is created by several stems which could reach at least 7 feet by rhizomes that are central to the plant. The thin and round stems are smooth on the bottom but slightly hairy at the top. Leaves alternate, with lance-shaped and have serrated margins. The tiny flowering yellow ones are located on top of the stems in races.

Parts that can be collected to use for medical reasons: leaves and flowers.

Most preferred solvent: water.

Main effect: Carminative, astringent, diaphoretic, diuretic.

Native American Use:

* Native Americans used the decoction made from Goldenrod leaves and flowers for treating a myriad of conditions. It was widely used to prevent illnesses like fever and colds. It was also found to be efficient in the case allergies to pollen or dust. It soothes the inflamed mucosae, and also to provide an effect of purification throughout the body (and kidneys, in particular) because of its powerful diuretic qualities.

This tea can be employed as a skin wash for wounds, ulcers, and cuts.

Flowers and leaves when dried, and then powdered were sprayed on topically to heal burns and wounds in order for a stoppage of bleeding. They also to absorb excessive water.

Goldenseal

Binomial Name: Hydrastis canadensis

The habitat is in the areas of well-drained forests in the Eastern United States and South-Eastern Canada. It is most often found in the vicinity of American Ginseng (Ashwagandha).

Specifications: This tiny flower can grow to 10 inches at the most and is found in dense populations in woodlands, specifically close to the American Ginseng. The plant grows from the underground rhizome and is a hairy plant with leaflets that are lobed (usually seven) that have serrated edges. The top part on the plant the flowers bloom in the spring. The flower is hermaphrodite with no petals and simply white stamens which surround the green calyx. The flowers will begin to fall shortly after blooming, allowing room to the round scarlet fruit that has shiny seeds of black.

Parts that are needed to be used for medical use such as Rhizome.

Most preferred solvents are water and alcohol.

Native American Use:

* Native Americans used the decoction of dried rhizomes as well as roots to treat dysentery, due to the specific characteristics of astringency. The decoction was also utilized to treat emollients and anti-inflammatory properties to be used as a rinse to treat skin inflammation and conjunctivitis. Consuming the raw root is believed to reap the benefits of these properties as well in treating sore throat and cough.

* Root extracts were frequently used to treat the condition scrofula as well as being a panacea for gallbladder and liver health issue.

* The dried rhizome powder could be applied to wounds and burns to stop the spread of infections because of its antiseptic characteristics. It was also regarded as an effective anti-fungal.

ADVICE: Consumption of this herb isn't permitted during lactation or pregnancy. Furthermore the excessive use of this herb could cause food poisoning.

Gooseberry

Binomial Name: Ribes uva crispa

Geographical location: in the forests that cover The Middle and Eastern areas of the North American continent. Both in the United States and Canada.

The characteristics of this many-branched perennial plant can reach at least 4 feet high and is widely spread throughout woodlands on ground that is low. The branches can bear or non-thorny parts on the same plant. They is surrounded with three- to five-lobed palmate leaves. The flowers that are green and white appear small tubes, which are placed together in clumps. Once pollinated the flowers develop into red, round and spiky fruit with a lot of brown-red seeds in.

Parts that should be collected for use in medical research: Fruits and roots.

Most preferred solvents are water and alcohol.

Native American Use:

In addition to the intake of fruit, Native Americans used the plants for medicinal purposes. The tea made from dried fruit was used to gargle for sore throats.

Also, the extract of the roots was utilized to wash the eyes irritation or drink directly because of its vermifuge properties to fight intestinal worms. In addition, the poultice composed comprised of leaves and fruit was applied to heal irritation to the skin because of its emollient properties. It was thought that it could cure snake bites due to the fact that snakes were scared of the leaves.

Gravel Root

Binomial Name: Eutrochium purpureum

Distribution: Widely distributed in humid environments in the Eastern region of North America, both in the United States and in Canada.

The characteristics of this perennial plant are that it may grow to up to 10 feet in height. The stems are straight out of the rhizome's central, underground part with many leaves that are arranged into groups of whorls. The leaves are striated and can be hairy to feel. On top of the stems are pink bell-shaped flowers are placed with umbrella-shaped groups.

Parts to be collected to use for medical reasons This includes the entire plant.

The preferred solvent is boiling water.

Effects: Diuretic, tonic, vermifuge, febrifuge.

Chapter 7: Hawthorn

Binomial Name: Crataegus laevigata

Dispersed in humid areas and in forests across The North American continent, both within both the United States and Canada.

Its characteristics: This plant is able to grow to 10 feet high in an intricate interlocking of branches. They are dense and thorny. filled with greenish yellowish leaves. 5-lobed, with serrated edges.

Parts to be collected to be used for medical reasons are leaves and fruit.

The preferred solvent is boiling water.

Native American Use:

* Natives utilized hawthorn leaves to treat minor cuts where no other remedy was readily available. Leaves could be chewed and the poultice was applied to burns and wounds to provide medical treatment during emergencies.

The plant was utilized to make decoctions from seeds, which could be used to treat diarrhea. The decoction also utilized to treat mild sedation, particularly in cases the heart was palpitating.

* The use for medical purposes of this plant has always been connected to heart disease in the eyes of Native Americans and, surprisingly numerous other populations from the past throughout the world. Recent research has proven that it is beneficial on heart diseases such that causes hypertension and tachycardia. Additionally, it could aid in lowering cholesterol levels.

ADVICE: Avoid consumption of this herb during lactation or pregnancy.

Heal-all

Binomial Name: Prunella vulgaris

It is found scattered across all over the United States and Canada in fields, meadows as well as at the edges of forest. It favors shady, moist areas.

Specifications: This tiny plant can reach 10 inches tall. It is a single horizontal stem, with the opposite leaves, oblong with sharp margins. The topmost part of the stem are blue/purple blooms arranged in the form of a whorled group.

Parts that are to be collected to use for medical reasons All the plant.

The preferred solvent is boiling water.

Effects: Hepatic, cholagogue, astringent.

Native American Use:

The name implies it was believed that Native Americans considered the plant to be a panacea against a variety of illnesses. The effects of tea produced by the plant in treating problems with gallbladder and liver is documented extensively in not just among Native Americans but also in various other societies around the globe. A lot of tribe healers used the herb and decoction because of its astringent properties, when it came to treating excessive menstrual cycle.

The other uses that have been documented for the decoction include such as mouthwashes to treat gingivitis and mouth sores and the use of it as a wash for burns and cuts, or in the form of a drink to help reduce diarrhea or fever attacks.

The raw consumption of this plant is helpful for sore throats.

Honeysuckle

Binomial Name: Lonicera japonica

Distribution: Spread across in the United States and Canada. Since it's invasive, it's often found in the fringes of streams and forests.

Specifications: This tiny plant is a climber. The leaves on the branches of green and red are oblong and shape like lances. The flowers have the form of trumpets of either red or white according to the species. They are adorned with exuding stamens of white or yellow. Fruit that results from pollination has a round shape and is black.

Parts that are to be collected to use for medical reasons This includes the entire plant.

The preferred solvent is boiling water or alcohol.

Effects: Febrifuge, astringent, antimicrobial.

Native American Use:

* Native Americans used the tea made from flowers for treating diarrhea and fever because of its astringent properties. This tea was employed as a gargle for the treatment of throat sores and laryngitis as well for a wash on the skin to treat common skin problems such as eczema or rash. The tea also could be used to treat of Urinary Tract Infections, and also to alleviate the signs of gonorrhea as well as Other Sexually Transmitted Diseases, like syphilis.

Hops

Binomial Name: Humulus lupulus

The location is within the inland region that is North West of the United States as well as South West of Canada.

The characteristics of this climbing perennial is the primary aromatic component when it comes to making beer. The green stems that climb are heavily populated with opposing leaves that have up to five lobes that have sharp edges. Female flowers are smaller and comprised of many florets and male flowers are yellow and small. Flowers of females transform into fruit (strobili) which have conical shape with grayish-yellowish colors.

Parts that can be collected for medical use female flowers.

The preferred solvent is boiling alcohol, water or diluted.

Effects: Diuretic, nervine, sedative, febrifuge.

Native American Use:

* Native Americans' medical use of hops isn't well-documented. Common herbal practices

recommend drinking the tea made from dried cones in order to lower the symptoms of fever and to calm nerves.

It is renowned for its use of leaves at the ceremony of sweat lodge.

WARNING: Hops may cause allergy.

Horsetail

The Binomial Name is Equisetum arvense

The location: It is scattered throughout all over the United States and southern Canada and along the shores of lakes.

The characteristics of this perennial are that it can be five feet tall. It has no leaves segmented, segmented plant with an apothecium at the top and spores are able to diffuse. It is in the summer that it appears to transform into a new type of plant. Many thin tall, needle-like branches develop to the stems with clusters.

Parts to be collected for use in medicine: Leaves and roots.

Most preferred solvent: water.

Effects: Emollient, astringent, diuretic.

Native American Use:

* Native Americans used this plant as a medicine for horses and humans. Actually, it's intriguing to remember the application of this plant to make a remedy to cure horses' cough.

* The principal medical reason for human beings was primarily due to diuretic properties that is why the tea brewed with needle-like roots was used for treating painful urinary tract infections when suffering from Sexual Transmitted Disease and Urinary Tract Infections all over the world. The bath that was created through the infusion of branches into hot water was utilized for treating gonorrhea as well as syphilis.

* The stem, which is reduced to a poultice utilized in applications to treat itchy skin.

Warning: Consumption of excessive amounts could cause poisoning.

Ironwood (Ocean Spray, Creambush)

Binomial Name: Holodiscus discolor

Distribution: Widely distributed across The Pacific Coast of the United States (especially in California) as well as Canada. The plant is able to grow in many habitats, ranging from coastal habitats that are moist to dry mountain environments.

Specifications: The shrub could grow to be anywhere from three to five feet high. It's got small, alternating leaves that are lance-shaped with edges that are serrated. Between May and July white, clumps of white delicately scented flowers fall at the edges of the branches. The fruits are tiny and surrounded with hair.

Parts that are needed to use for medical reasons: Flowers and leaves.

The preferred solvent is water.

Effects: Astringent.

Native American Use:

* * The Lummi tribe that lived in the Northern region of Washington State, near Bellingham utilized the concoction of flowers in order to prevent diarrhoea.

* British Columbia Natives used attributed to berries decoction to achieve the same goal as well as using the berries as a cleanser in the case of chickenpox and smallpox for children.

The poultice made of leaves was utilized for treating burns and wounds.

Juniper

Binomial Name: Juniperus comunis

The location is widely distributed all across throughout the North American continent, both within the United States and Canada

The characteristics of this evergreen tree could reach at least 50 feet in its prime. Thorn-like leaves that are arranged in whorls are abundantly spotted on these branches tree. The female flowers are tiny with a spherical shape and are in green. Male flowers are tiny, yellow and develop in clusters of three. They are shaped like a catkin that is adorned with stamens. Highly aromatic berries deep blue and tough.

Parts that can be collected to use for medical reasons for medical purposes: Berries.

Most preferred solvents: Boiling alcohol or water.

Native American Use:

* In addition to the extensively documented usage of dried berries for spice used to flavor game meat and other game meats, the plant was extensively used for medical uses, not just by indigenous peoples, but also by Mediterranean culture.

* For instance the decoction derived from the berries could aid with dysmenorrhea and premenstrual symptoms. It was also utilized for its diuretic and antiseptic properties for

treating Urinary Gallbladder Infections as well as tract issues. The bark and needles can be added to the mixture to increase the effectiveness.

ADVICE: Avoid consumption of this herb while pregnant or during lactation or in cases renal diseases.

Lady's Slipper

Binomial Name: Cypripedioideae

The location: It is found in moist areas all across all of the Northern United States and Canada.

Particularities: From the single stem of this annual plant numerous stems may grow to three feet high. Each stem features basal similar leaflets that are lance-shaped. The leaves are paler shades in green lower side than on the top and are up to one foot in length. The top flower is pale pink and resembles a slipper orchid.

Effects: Astringent, antiperiodic.

The parts to be collected to use for medical reasons Parts to collect for medical purposes: Root.

The preferred solvent is boiling water or alcohol.

Native American Use:

* Native Americans collected the rhizome from this plant for therapeutic purpose, mostly in autumn, when it was planned in the process of letting the leaf and stem drop off for winter. The best time to gather all types of taproots, roots and rhizomes as all medicinal substances be concentrated on them because of the proximity of winter.

The best methods to get the most efficiency using Lady's Slipper roots is the decoction, and tincture. The two preparations were employed to treat dysentery as well as diarrhea as well as to decrease fever. Additionally, they had a relaxing affect on nerves.

Chapter 8: Lemon Balm

Binomial Name: Melissa officinalis

The location: It is found throughout gardens and meadows across Canada and the United States and Canada.

The characteristics of this perennial low-lying shrub grows to about 3 inches in height. It is rooted through a variety of stems, each with bright, oval-shaped leaves that have edges that are serrated. The flowers are tiny in size, round and white. One of the main characteristics that this flower has is its powerful scent of lemon which radiates from flowers and leaves which is why it's called.

Effects: Carminative, febrifuge, analgesic.

Parts to be collected to use for medical reasons: leaves flowering, stems, and leaves.

Most preferred solvents: Boiling alcohol, water.

Native American Use:

* Native Americans used the tea made from the aerial parts of the plant due to the numerous benefits it offered. Lemon balm were helpful in reducing gastric. In addition, its analgesic properties helped to soothe nerves as well as, when combined with the anticonvulsant compounds in it, aids in treating menstrual cramps. In addition, the diaphoretic chemicals in it trigger sweat and encourage cleansing of the body as well as a reduction of body temperature when there is a cases of fever that is excessive.

This is a great plant for people with black thumbs as it can be very infesting, and quite difficult to eradicate. It can cover the entire surface it can and it is recommended to cultivate to plant it in pots within your house. The harvesting time of lemon balm occurs in spring, for leaves, and the summer months for blooms.

Licorice (Wild American)

Binomial Name: Glycyrhizza lepidota

Locality: widely diffused throughout the moist and humid environments in Canada or the Western United States or Canada.

The plant's characteristics are that it grows with intricate root stalks that is spread across the width, rather than increasing in the height. Flat, oblong leaves with sleek edges adorn the stalks of roots and towards the top on the stem, green yellowish blooms are in groups that are vertical, similar to clover. The seeds are housed in pods like peas and have a glossy black.

Effects: Emollient, purgative, expectorant, febrifuge.

The parts to be collected for use in medical research: the roots (dried) and the leaves.

The preferred solvent is water.

Native American Use:

* Native Americans widely used the liquorice to treat medical conditions mostly related to stomach issues. Actually, the tea made from

the peeled and dried roots was utilized as a laxative in the event constipation. Another reason to drink the tea was to lower fever as the diaphoretic compounds that are present in the tea induce sweating on the sufferer.

* The other medical benefits of wild licorice associated with the tea from leaves that were used as a treatment for earache that is applied to the skin, and raw root consumption to relieve sore throats and toothaches.

The poultice made from the fresh root was applied topically to joints with swelling, in cases of gout or rheumatism.

ADVICE: It can increase blood pressure. Therefore, it is not recommended in the case of hypertension.

Mayapple

Binomial Name: Podophyllum peltatum

Dispersed within the forests of Canada and the Eastern United States and Canada.

The characteristics of this perennial flower are that it thrives in the thick woodlands that are shaded and arid. Every stout is adorned with two broad leaflets and five lobes. The one flower that develops under those leaves, is yellow includes six petals, surrounded by the central cluster of stamens in yellow. The edible fruit is ripe at the end of the summer.

Effects: Purgative, cholagogue.

Items to gather for use in medicine Roots and sap.

Most preferred solvents: Boiling the alcohol and water.

Native American Use:

* Native Americans used Mayapple roots applied topically to treat wounds or powder for treating warts. The decoction derived from the leaves can be a powerful laxative as well as an emetic, and it could be used for treating intestinal worms.

Note: Root decoction could be utilized as a potent organic insecticide in your garden.

ADVICE: Only use under the supervision of a medical professional.

Maple

Binomial Name: Acer.

Habitat: Common tree extensively distributed across this North American continent.

Specifications: This group of deciduous trees comprises a variety of species, whose heights can differ dramatically, ranging from 30 feet to 150 feet high. In all species, the bark can be wrinkled on older trees, whereas it appears smoother in the younger plants. Leaves are numerous, with three lobes and have sharp edges. Samaras are fruits, which are winged achenes that has vertical "leaflets" such as helicopter blades. They help seeds travel long distances once they break off to the trees.

The parts to be collected to use for medical reasons: The inner branches and leaf.

Most preferred solvent: Boiling water.

Effects: Astringent.

Native American Use:

* Native Americans widely used the maple for their daily life. Actually, the sap was the most potent sugar source available to the people. The sap was collected during the winter months and in spring, and utilized to sweeten their diets. This same method is used in the present day for processing and harvesting of maple syrup.

Apart from the nutrition it also served to treat ailments: The leaves infusion was utilized to cleanse the body, and the inside bark decoction could be used to wash to treat conjunctivitis as well as other eye issues. In the event of drinking, the bark decoction can have an expectorant action, which aids to eliminate the phlegm from a cases of sore throat and cough. throat.

Milkweed

Binomial Name: Asclepias speciosa

Disperses mostly around the agricultural fields. It is found throughout the North American continent, both within Canada and in the United States and Canada.

Specifications: This perennial plant develops from one stem rising from the ground and reaching about three or five feet high. Leaves are oblong, opposite and oval in shape. Pink flowers are arranged in spherical clusters which grow out of the leaf edges. Seeds are housed in seedpods and are surrounded by a pappus, which can be easily moved by winds.

The parts to be collected for medical use The following are the most common: leaves, flowers, and the roots.

The preferred solvent is boiling water.

Native American Use:

* Native Americans used milkweed flowers exclusively after careful preparation due to their rich amount of poisonous compounds

(cardiac glycosides). The flowers were eaten when they were cooked. Seeds were crushed into flour for bread making.

* The medicinal uses of this plant are numerous including the preparation of dried roots for lactation enhancement to the topically applied application of sap released from leaves for treating warts, insect bites, and urticaria.

The poultice from leaves was utilized for wound treatment and the leaves that were dried infusion was used for stomach issues.

ADVICE: It is not recommended to use it with no medical supervision or advice due to the toxic ingredients that can harm the heart. The use of this product can cause infertility.

Mullein

The Binomial Name is Verbascum thapsus.

Habitat: A common plant that is widely spread across the mountains in Canada and the United States and Canada, from coast to coast.

Particulars: Mullein is an annual straight plant that is up to 8 feet tall. Its single stem is covered by leaves which grow in groups all around the stem. The lower leaves are large as well as long and hairy. The size of the leaves decreases from lower to the highest point in the stem. The top of the spike is an upward-facing flower cluster that is yellow and has pistils of red.

Parts to be collected for medical use such as leaves and flowers.

Most preferred solvent: Boiling water.

Effects: Emollient, diuretic, astringent.

Native American Use:

The demulcent effects of Mullein (leaves as well as flowers) was well-known to Native Americans who used it in teas and decoctions to treat respiratory issues of a mild nature including nasal congestion.

Mullein's action was usually coupled with other herbs like thyme or rosemary.

*The poultice made from leaves that were fresh was applied to treat swellings, wounds as well as skin conditions like rashes. dried leaves were burned to cause coughing and help relieve the cough.

Note: Mullein is particularly indicated for gardeners with little experience due to its ability to grow in the yard.

Oak

Binomial Name: Quercus.

Area: Widely distributed across in the United States and Canada, from coast to coast in the woods and yards.

Specifications: This group includes numerous species of trees which may grow to 100 feet. The leaves on their branches massive trees have a variety of alternative. Cuts, edges and the overall appearance of leaves vary between species. In all plant, male flowers appear as pink amentia, while female flowers are tiny and green. They are situated at the bottom on the leaf. When pollinated, they transform into the acorns.

Parts that can be collected to use for medical reasons such as acorns and barks.

The preferred solvent is boiling water.

Effects: Antiseptic, astringent.

Native American Use:

* Native Americans' use of the oak was for for sustenance and medical reasons. Acorns were ground into a food-grade paste as well as tea taken from the barks was used for an ointment to treat mouth sores (mouth gum sores and gum inflammation) also for cuts and burns generally.

* The powdered and dried bark was utilized as an antiseptic to be applied topically application on the wounds to speed up the healing process.

* The the red oak bark was used to treat abdominal pain.

* The medical benefits associated with oak stem from the high amount of tannins, Astringent chemical compound that can be utilized to treat a variety of digestive disorders as well as to ease digestive discomfort.

Oregon Grape

Binomial Name: Mahonia aquifolium

The location is a wide-spread evergreen tree dispersed at the edges of forests in the northwestern United States.

The characteristics of this evergreen plant could grow up to seven feet high. Leaves are sharp, pinnate and brilliant green. Flowers are small, yellowish-greenish with sepals of purple and develop to blueberries following pollination. The roots are bright yellow within.

Chapter 9: Passionflower

Binomial Name: Passiflora

The location is mostly diffused along wooded edges in the south-eastern US.

Specifications: This plant can reach as high as forty feet in the height. The stems that grow from the roots are reddish brown with alternating light hairy leaves that have sharp margins. The flowers are huge and clearly identified by the blue-white top of blooms near the prominent pistils.

Parts that can be collected to treat medical conditions: Leaves and flowers.

The preferred solvent is alcohol.

Effects: Sedative, diuretic, analgesic.

Native American Use:

* Native Americans used the tea made from dried or fresh flowers and leaves to induce a gentle, calming tranquilizer. It was beneficial for gastric pain and stomach discomfort and also served to treat menstrual cramps.

Infusions of crushed root was utilized to treat earache as well as on topically applied applications against hemorrhoids. The poultice from the root could be applied topically on cuts as well as skin irritations.

Peppermint

Binomial Name: Mentha piperita

The location: It is diffused across all over the United States and Canada, usually near rivers and pound.

Specifications: This tiny plant grows from the rhizome's base as a straight stem that has a square segment and has many lance-shaped leaves. They are vibrant fresh, fragrant with serrated margins. These tiny flowers form clusters on the upper part of the plant, in diverse colors, dependent on the kind of plant (white for peppermint, blue or violet for different varieties that are mint).

Parts that can be collected for use in medicine: Leaves and stems.

Most preferred solvents are alcohol and water.

Effects: Carminative, stimulant.

Native American Use:

* Native Americans' use as the food source of peppermint has been well recorded.

* The medical side is not as well-known. The tea that is made of fresh or dried leaves aids people with gastric issues due to the presence of the carminative compounds that are present in the tea.

Essential oil effective as a stimulant. It can be utilized to relax muscles that are sore because of its cooling effects upon the body.

* In the ceremony at sweat lodge the leaves were dripped over hot stones to provide effective treatment against airway congestions.

The poultice is used as a treatment for burning skin and other ailments such as the urticarial.

Beware: essential oils may be abrasive to heal burns and open wounds.

Tips for Beginner GARDENERS Mint is extremely Infesting. Plant them inside steel containers, otherwise your garden will be infested.

Plantain

Binomial Name: Plantago lanceolata or marittima

Disperses all across throughout the United States, alongside cultivated fields as well as along the coast to it to be called the Plantago marittima.

Specifications: This tiny species emerges from its soil as an upright, long green stem. Leaves are of different shapes and styles depending to the species. The Lanceolata species is characterized by oblong pointed leaves. While the Marittima leaves are sharper. An upward-facing spike of tiny hermaphrodite blooms compose the inflorescence. Each flower features protruding stamens that have hair-like, thin pedicles.

Parts that can be collected to use for medical reasons: leaves and stems.

The preferred solvent is water.

Effects: Astringent, antiseptic.

Native American Use:

* Native Americans used Plantain both as a food source and also for medicinal reasons. The leaves were eaten for food but were it was not very nutritious.

* Tea made from flowers produces a gel-like beverage which is used for treating diarrhea and dysentery. It helps to ease spasmic attacks as well as soothe an inflamed digestive. Additionally, the poultice created through chewing the fresh leaf of the freshly cut plant was applied to the skin to treat skin and urticarial inflammations, and is also used to treat antiseptic injuries.

* The freshly cut leaves were dried out in summer, and were all through the year particularly during colder seasons for treating coughs and colds since the tea made from it is a potent diuretic and expectorant.

* Last but not least, the pure consumption of seeds was utilized for constipation cases because of its powerful the laxative effects.

Prickly Pear

Binomial Name: Opuntia

Disperses throughout dry regions across all over the Southern United States, alongside cultivable fields.

Its characteristics: This plant is part of the cactus family and is characterized by large, drop-shaped lighter green pads that are covered in black dots. From these thorns, the thorns appear. The flowers are huge and yellow. Fruits have egg-like shapes and come in a variety of shades inside one plant (yellow as well as purple, green as well as orange).

Parts that should be collected for medical use: Pads fruit, flowers, and pads.

Most preferred solvent: water.

Effects: Astringent, antiseptic.

Native American Use:

* The Native Americans from in the Southern States widely used pads as well as flowers and fruits to eat (after peeling, naturally).

* The therapeutic benefits of this well-known Cactus are not as well-known. The tea derived from the flowers has astringency and can be beneficial for those suffering from irritable bowel disorder and dysentery. It helps calm diarrhea that is agitated and to ease the swelling inside. A different use for the plant is the topical application of peeling pads to burns and injuries to reduce infection and promote healing. A lesser-known use for the peeled pads is its application of the pads on the breasts using a topical cream to encourage the lactation process.

Purslane

Binomial Name: Portulaca oleracea

The location is widely distributed all across in the United States and Canada, in meadows, gardens and gardens.

The characteristics of this small succulent plant can be that is often seen in every garden. The stems are red/purple and emerge from the soil in an intricate knot and grow anywhere. The leaves that surround the stems are slender, pointed and with a smooth edge. These flowers, either orange or yellow feature five heart-shaped, vibrant petals that surround an explosion of stamens protruding. They bloom during the month of June.

Parts that are to be collected for medical use All the plant.

Most preferred solvent: water.

Native American Use:

* Native Americans used this small flower in a manner similar as the evening primrose in

which the entire plant was pounded for poultice. It was utilized to treat skin ailments such including eczemas or urticaria or for aiding to heal injuries. The juice that was obtained from squeezed this poultice in cheesecloth sheets was applied topically to treat earache.

* The plant's fresh leaves were additionally used to be a wash applied topically for burns and wounds because of its antiseptic qualities and as a drink that could be used to combat intestinal worms. The only decoction made of leaves proved to be emollient and stringent to the stomach, and it was extensively used for diarrhea treatment.

Red Clover

Binomial Name: Trifolium pratense

Dispersed throughout across the United States, in sunny plains and meadows.

The characteristics of this perennial plant grows from a single stem with hairs that emerges from the ground. It is able to reach up to twenty inches tall. The compound leaves that alternate are trifoliate. The lower compound is characterized by large petioles that are not present in the higher compound. The leaves are oval as well as hairy with the smooth edges. The leaves have the distinctive arrow-tip "stain" of light green towards the middle. It ends by forming a spherical clump of purple or red tubular flowering in July through September.

Parts that can be collected for medical use: leaves and flowers.

Effects: Expectorant.

Native American Use:

* Native Americans used red clover tea for tonic purposes as well as for respiratory ailments, including asthma and cough. Furthermore, this tea was utilized as a cleanser for burns and cuts because of its astringent properties and also as a treatment for womenopausal-related side effects, including especially hot flashes. The

diaphoretic effects is a great aid in cleansing the body. It also regulates thyroid hormone production which causes chills and hot flashes.

ADVICE: If consumed as part of menstrual cycle, it can lead to excessive bleeding. Therefore drinking should be taken in consultation with a physician specialist.

Redroot

Binomial Name: Ceanothus

The location is scattered across all over the Western States of the whole North American continent, from the Pacific Ocean to the Rocky Mountains and from California all the way to British Columbia.

Specifications: This plant comes in nearly forty species. It is primarily the ground-covering plant in large expanses, but it may differ based upon the type of plant. As an example, Ceanothus americana is a smaller plant that is between six and eight feet high.

The stems are adorned with tiny thorns, and they have flowers of white (or blue) flower groups at the ends. Seeds are small and triangular, and are packed into pods. The medical component is called the root. The outside of the root is dark black, but after removal, it shows the inner root in red. The time to harvest the root typically falls during the fall season. It is important to slice and peel the root after it has been fresh since after drying, it turns very hard.

Parts that are needed to use for medical reasons The root.

Effects: Expectorant, Astringent, sedative, febrifuge.

Native American Use:

* Native Americans used redroot decoction to ease sore throats particularly newborns. The sedative properties that the plant has helped with decreasing the discomfort associated with tonsillitis. Its expectorant action helped in removing the phlegm and speed

recuperation from illness. The decoction of the root was efficient in relieving fever the sweat-inducing ingredients (diaphoretic) as well as stimulating the lymphatic system as well as the immune system.

* The most effective method of assuming that the root is through taking the tincture. Drinking between 20 and 30 drops and let them "drip" throughout the tonsils and throughout the throat can provide relief for the throat that is sore and speedy recovery.

Romero

Binomial Name: Thricostema ianatum

It can be found throughout the Southern portion of California and along the Pacific coastline of Mexico.

Its characteristics: This plant is as high as five feet at the base, with multiple complex branches. The leaves are tiny and pointed, similar to rosemary. It was misinterpreted by the early conquistadores. From March through June, the plant blossoms with small clusters of either purple or blue in a goblet shape, that have three petals, and prominent purple stamens.

Parts to be collected for medical use including leaves and flowers.

Effects: Expectorant, febrifuge, anticonvulsant, analgesic.

Native American Use:

* Native Americans mainly used the Romero to treat their anxiety due to its anticonvulsant qualities. The decoction from Romero leaves can help soothe stomach upsets and ease menstrual cramps. Additionally, when drunk regularly, the drink has positive effects for sore joints as well as muscle discomfort and can enhance your cardiovascular system as a result of the expansion capillary sections.

Chapter 10: Sassafras

Binomial Name: Sassafras albidum

Area: Edges and Meadows of forest areas in the Eastern and Midwestern United States. The forest needs dry places for growth and to thrive.

Specifications: The tree could reach up to fifty feet in height. Its leaves are trilobed, with an irregular edge. The roots have been utilized as natural scents in a variety of drinks and beverages, for instance the root beer. In reality, broken roots are smell the same as. They are greenish yellowish and have six petals, which are surrounded by the crown with yellow pistils.

Items to gather for medical use: root branches, barks, leaves.

Native American Use:

* Native Americans used the dried leaves to make a spice either by grinding them or crushing the leaves.

* The decoction made from roots is used for tonic, and also for its cleansing effects. Additionally, it can bring some relief from sexual transmitted diseases like syphilis, or the gonorrhoea. The anticonvulsant properties of this root extract can also be a beneficial treatment of menstrual pain, stomachache as well as cramps.

* Bark tea was employed for its diaphoretic benefits to act as a potent febrifuge.

ADVICE: Sassafras roots produce a substance called safrole that can cause cancer. Because of this, it should be consumed in conjunction with a physician and under the supervision of a physician.

Saint John's Wort

Binomial Name: Hypericum perforatum

Distribution: Widely distributed throughout in the United States and Canada, in meadows, gardens and other areas.

Specifications: This mystical, perennial can reach about four feet in height by the rhizome that creeps. The red-brown stems have hardy in the middle of the plant. They grow increasingly "tender" towards the top of the plant. The stalkless and opposite leaves are found on the branches. They're large and bright green and have many glands that are attached to the base. They are easily visible through the backlight. Flowers that begin at the ends of each stem are created by five yellow petals which are surrounded by a row of pistils that are long and yellow. Seeds are glossy black and cylindrical with a length of two millimeters.

Parts that are to be collected for medical use This includes the entire plant.

Native American Use:

* Native Americans were aware of its benefits and frequently employed it in various remedies. The plant was believed to be a healing plant that had anti-inflammatory, astringent and antiseptic properties.

The whole decoction of the plant was used to treat estrogenic properties that helped treat issues with menstrual flow, for example low blood flow, or Pre-Menstrual Syndrome. The stimulant effect on the contraction of the uterus was utilized to induce abortions as well as help with difficult childbirth.

This is not all, the tea made from flowers could be used for a mild sedative that helped soothe nerves and help induce sleeping in the event of trauma incidents or sleeplessness.

For applications of fresh plants you can think of the poultice that was made of the entire plant was applied to the wound to speed healing and prevent infections because of the antiseptic qualities of this plant. Additionally, the raw root consumption was utilized to treat snake bites. In addition, flowers and leaves were utilized raw to help heal nasal epistaxis and wounds since they stopped the bleeding immediately.

Warning: Do not consume during pregnancy or when you are suffering with depression or bipolar disorder.

Side effects The most common side effects are irritation to the stomach or allergic reactions.

Saw Palmetto

Binomial Name: Serenoa repens

The location is scattered across the United States, especially in the South-Eastern region. The majority of it grows in large colonies in plains and sandhills. It is particularly prevalent close to the coast. The plant can also be found in woodlands beneath pines.

Specifications: This palm is sometimes referred to as Dwarf American Palm and can be up to 13 feet high at its highest. The central trunk is deep scaled, are a variety of leaves that are arranged with a large petiole filled with thorns along its sides. It ends with a fan of ten up to 20 leaflets. Leaflets range from two up to three feet long, and sharp. Flowers in vertical panicles featuring three white petals as well as six yellow stamens are visible between the leaflets in the spring. They are large, black or red drupes similar to the size of an olive.

Parts to be collected for medical use leaves.

Native American Use:

* Native Americans used palm leaves for building materials for roofs on basic shelters. In terms of medical benefits of palm leaves, the most important thing to mention was the decoction made from leaves to treat digestive disorders and lower the severity of fever.

Modern Use:

* Saw palmetto is lately studied in the treatment of prostate cancer as well as prostate signs of enlargement. The consumption of Saw Palmetto regulates the

production of testosterone, thereby reducing the potential for prostate cells to reproduce. The majority of food supplements that you can find in the pharmacy have their roots in Saw Palmetto extraction.

Senega Snakeroot

Binomial Name: Poligala senega

The location is scattered across the Eastern up to the Central United States and Canada all the way from New Scotland to Saskatchewan, up to Mississippi State to South Carolina.

Specifications: This tiny flower has a life cycle and is perennial. At the base, every year, many stems break out and reach 15 inches. They are smooth and red and have points-shaped lances that spirally placed. On the highest point of the stem, white flowers form horizontal, densely packed groupings.

The parts to be collected to use for medical reasons The root.

Most preferred solvents: water Alcohol, water.

Effects: Expectorant, febrifuge.

Native American Use:

* Ojibwa employed this plant along with others in the preparation of a cure-all mostly used by warriors. The combination of herbs supposed to strengthen and aid in healing. Ojibwa warriors would chew regularly and rub the mixture on burns and wounds. The plant was also utilized during ceremonies, and it was believed to possess the ability to ward off evil spirits.

* The powder of dried roots is applied to wounds to aid in healing due to its antiseptic and astringent qualities.

Consuming raw root is suggested in cases of cough. It can aid in exhalation of the phlegm as well as during fever episodes because of its diaphoretic qualities.

* The poultice made of root may be sprayed over the area of swelling, and is very beneficial in decreasing swelling.

Slippery Elm

Binomial Name: Ulmus rubra.

The location is widely distributed throughout fields and forests across Canada, including the North-Eastern United States and Quebec.

Particularities: The deciduous trees could grow to as high as 50 feet in an average. Leaves spread wide within the central trunk that is composed from reddish-colored wood. These dark-green leaves are oval to oval-shaped (depending upon the type) and feature serrated margins. They're rough to surface in the upper portion as well as soft on the lower. The flowers have no petals. They come in clusters ranging from 15 to 20 each. They are ovoid samaras, which are quickly diffused by winds and carry a red hairy seed.

Parts to be collected to use for medical reasons The Bark is both the inner and out.

The most preferred solvents are water, alcohol.

Effects: Expectorant, emollient, diuretic.

Native American Use:

* The Native Americans extensively utilized this indigenous species of elm for its medicinal uses using a mixture of the dry bark. The bark's inner layer releases a muclaginous compound that, when consumed, may help to treat ulcers and gastritis by shielding stomach walls. It can also be utilized as a cleanser, it's an effective emollient to heal burns and cuts. Similar effects can be obtained through the infusion of inside bark that was powdered.

* The bark extract was utilized in a different way to trigger the contraction of the uterus and also to trigger abortions or assist with difficult childbirths.

* The solution obtained from adding beeswax to the bark's oil can be used to fight colds, sore throat and bronchitis. This is accomplished through dissolving by boiling it in water, and then taking in it with smoke (fumigation).

Stinging Nettle

Binomial Name: Urtica dioica

It is widely distributed over United States and Canada, in close proximity to cultivated fields, marshes and all wetlands.

Specifications: This perennial can reach at least five feet due to the rhizome's creeping. One stem, with an oval section is smothered by stinging hair. The leaves are dark green ovate, opposite and have deeply serrated margins. Female and male flowering plants have four petals that protect the organs of reproduction (stamens or ovaries). Female flowers develop after pollination, which is carried out in an egg-shaped achene.

The parts to be taken for use in medical research: Roots and leaves.

Most preferred solvent: Boiling water.

Effects: Diuretic, astringent, expectorant.

Native American Use:

* Native Americans widely used the net to treat various ailments associated with the upper respiratory tract. There is ample evidence that infusions of fresh leaves and stems can be used to treat coughs, allergies as well as asthmatic disorders.

Chapter 11: Sumac

Binomial Name: Rhus coriaria

The location: Sumac thrives in forests as well as fields across the United States, especially in the south-eastern region.

Its characteristics: This plant can be at least 30 feet tall in the rhizome that is underground. The branches twist out from the ground, and then spread with a variety of smaller red-brownish branches. The leaves are compound in shape, in the shape of a lance, and vibrant green, with serrated edges. Five petals of red flowers are laid out in the form of vertical panicles and are densely packed with. Following pollination, the flowers transform into drupes in red.

Parts to be collected to use for medical reasons The Bark is both the inner and out.

The most preferred solvents are water and alcohol.

Effects: Astringent, anti-inflammatory.

Native American Use:

* Native Americans used the decoction of sumac as cleanser to treat conjunctivitis, and also as a gargle to relieve sore throats. It was also consumed in order to take advantage of its astringent qualities in cases of dysentery or diarrhea.

The freshly cut leaves were crushed to form an anti-inflammatory poultice used to treat the urticarial and skin rash using a topical application.

Tobacco

Binomial Name: Nicotiana

The habitat is wild throughout areas of the South-Western United States, in areas of desert.

Specifications: This plant could grow to 13 feet high. The leaves can be described as lanceolate (typical dimensions include 12 inches in length and 4 inches wide at its bottom) as well as yellow-greenish. Leaf dimensions decrease from lower to the base. Flowers are in the upper part of the plant they are trumpet-shaped, pink and. They emit a sour taste.

Parts that are collected to be used for medical reasons leaves.

Preferred Solvents: Water.

Effects: Antispasmodic, cathartic, emetic, analgesic.

Native American Use:

* Native Americans used tobacco mainly to perform rituals by inhaling pipes for sacred purposes. Also, the plant was used in small amounts for medical use to treat pain. Actually, the poultice derived from pounding fresh leaves was applied to joints that were swelling or scorpion stings in order to lessen the pain as well as to be an effective treatment for skin problems. Powdered or fresh leaves were chewed for relief from headaches.

* Lastly, when combined together with chalk, leaves' poultice could be used as a prehistoric tooth paste to lighten the teeth.

Toothwort

Binomial Name: Cardamine Diphylla.

It is found in the humid woodlands of Quebec and the Eastern United States and Quebec.

Specifications: The plant is part of the mustard family, and therefore it can be eaten. Its single, thin stem, that may grow as high as twelve" tall, is adorned with leaves that are lance-shaped with serrated edges that are arranged into triplets. The topmost part of the plant are a few white flowers, each with four petals.

Parts to be collected for medical use Parts to collect for medical purposes: Roots.

Preferred Solvents: Water.

Effects: Febrifuge, analgesic, carminative.

Native American Use:

* Algonquin Native Americans widely used the roots of this tiny flower to treat ailments. The root infusion was utilized for fever reduction and also as a gargle used to treat sore throats, particularly in young children. This infusion also served to treat the symptoms associated with sexually transmitted diseases like Gonorrhea and Syphilis. Additionally, the roots were consumed in raw form by just chewing it in order to relieve headaches because of its analgesic qualities and also to decrease stomach gas (carminative impact). The poultice of the root was also used to treat swellings and arthritis joints.

Usnea

Binomial Name: Usnea

The habitat of wild lichen is in moist conditions, particularly within the North-Western United States and British Columbia.

The characteristics of this lichen are that it is a symbiont found in the junipers, pines, cypresses among others. It grows on the branches, and feeds on tree's lymphatic system, allowing it to exchange nitrogenous compounds. It's easy to identify the Usnea (also known as "old man's beard"): Usnea has a white central core that is the source of the numerous filaments. Some lichens that could contain poisonous substances do not have this white central axon make sure you check prior to picking poisonous clones.

Parts of lichen to be collected for use in medical research Whole the lichen.

Preferred Solvents: Water.

Effects: Carminative, antiseptic, emollient, antifungal.

Native American Use:

* Cowichan tribe of The South Western part of Canada employed the poultice from the entire lichen to treat wounds and skin inflammations. The powdered and dried lichen was applied in a similar method to soak up the fluid flowing from burns and injuries as

well as to speed healing by relying on its antiseptic capabilities.

Alcoholic tinctures made from lichen can be used for treating diseases (pulmonary particularly like tuberculosis). The raw drink or tea made from dried lichen is utilized in the same manner as.

* The tea is utilized to wash the vagina can effectively treat any yeast or fungal infection including candida.

Valerian

A Binomial Name is Valeriana officinalis

The location of this plant is due to the climate of mountains. It's usually on the northern slopes of the mountains, and in the hills throughout Canada and the United States and Canada.

The characteristics of this small plant can grow to nearly sixty inches. Its roots emerge from the ground and form a single, green stem with nodes that appear at regular intervals. At each node, two branches that are opposite and bear between seven and nine lance-shaped and smooth-edged leaves. The top is divided into three lower vertical branches, with a clump of white, small flowers at the the top. The flowers are bell-shaped and have four white petals, and the central stamen protrudes. They bloom from April until July.

The parts to be collected to use for medical reasons The root.

Preferred Solvents: Water.

Effects: Sedative, Nervine.

Native American Use:

* Valerian is well-known not just by Native Americans but also among numerous ancient peoples because of its sedative properties. The tea made using Valerian roots can be described as an eminently sedative stress relieving beverage. It promotes sleep and therefore it can be beneficial in treating insomnia. Another benefit of the root

decoction is its astringency. which is why this extract was used for treating colds and diarrhea.

* The poultice made from roots is a great option for treating burns, wounds as well as skin irritation generally.

* The effects of this herb can be increased when combined with other plants including peppermint red clover, and gentian.

Venus's Slipper

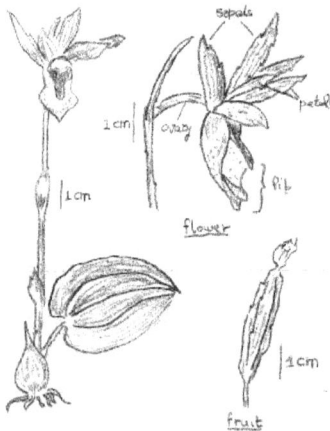

Binomial Name: Calypso bulbosa

The location of this mountain plant is widespread throughout both the United States and Canada, especially in humid environments.

The characteristics of this plant is known as a slipper that is able to grow up to 10 inches tall. It is a single broad basal leaf that is with a pointed lance, shaped like a lance, as well as bright green. On the upper part of the plant, the plant is blooms during March, turning as an orchid, with prominent pink and purple petals. Labellum refers to the protuberance of purple that runs down the middle of the flower. It's similar as a slipper.

Chapter 12: Violet

Binomial Name: Viola odorata

The location is widely distributed all across Canada and the United States and Canada, in moist woodlands and shady habitats.

The characteristics: Perennial small plant that may grow as tall as 10 inches when at its peak. Its leaves are heart-shaped, with sharp margins, and are displaced to form an apical the rosette. When the season is over, winter, it blossoms with small, violet blooms with five petals that are zygomorphic.

Parts to be collected to use for medical reasons such as leaves and flowers.

Most preferred solvent: Boiling water.

Main effect: Antibacterial, expectorant, carminative, laxative.

Native American Use:

* Native Americans used violet as healing plant. Teas made from violet were used to regulate body functions and in reducing gastric acid thanks to its carminative characteristics. Additionally, it was believed to be beneficial in cooling the body.

* Infusing the infusion with dried flowers is believed to help reduce chronic mucus production. This includes earaches, sore throats, hoarseness, cough and so on.

Watercress

A Binomial Name Nasturtium officinalis

Its habitat: The wild species thrives in humid habitats like marshes and bogs across Canada and the United States and Canada.

Specifications: The plant is cultivated in mats that are floating, and the roots are that are submerged into the water. It expands in width rather than growing in height. and can grow to twenty inches when in height at its highest. The plant is an intricate intertwined entanglement of stems that have alternate three-lobed ovate leaves. In the months of May through July near the top of stems, tiny clusters of 3 to 5 white flowers blossom.

Parts that can be collected for use in medical research: Roots and leaves.

Preferred Solvents: Water.

Effects: Detoxifying, carminative.

Native American Use:

* The best-documented utilization of this plant among Native Americans is the use of

leaves for spice in the food they ate due to their hot and pungent taste.

* Medical use isn't as well known, and suggests that the plant is consumed in its raw form. plant for treating coughs or colds as well as digestion due to its potent expectorant properties. The expectorant and astringent properties are a great help in the elimination of phlegm and excess mucus quickly.

* It also is a powerful diuretic which was used for detoxification and cleansing.

Tips for the Beginner GARDENER The plant is able to quickly grow in your backyard by removing it from the ground and then replanting it. Make sure you provide enough water.

Water Birch

Binomial Name: Betula occidentalis

The location is widely distributed in the interior regions of the Western United States and Canada and Canada, all the way up to the eastern portion of Alaska.

The characteristics of this small tree may grow 35 to 35 feet high With many trunks arising that originate from a single rootstock. The branches (covered by a red-brown, smooth bark) are separated by several branches that are populated by opposing oval leaves that have edges that are serrated. The flowers are catkins, the male drooping and the females standing up. Seeds are the horizontal "leaflets" such as a helicopter (samara). They can fly lengthy distances once they separate away from their tree.

Parts to be collected to use for medical reasons: leaves and bark.

Most preferred solvents are alcohol and water.

Main effect: Anti-inflammation, febrifuge.

Native American Use:

* Native Americans used the Water Birch febrifuge properties to make the strongest tea with the bark and leaves. The drink can be utilized as a cleanser for skin conditions that are mild including pimples.

WARNING: Do not use during pregnancy.

Willow

Binomial Name: Salix alba

The habitat is widely distributed in moist areas across the North American Continent, both within Canada and in the United States and Canada.

Specifications: The tree could reach at least 100 feet in height. From the broad central trunk, branch out several drooping branches that are surrounded with lance-shaped and narrow leaves adorned with serrated edges. The downward-sloping form of its branches give the tree its unique form. Flowers for males and female, are in the form of catkins. Yellow for males and green for females.

Parts that can be collected for medical use Parts to collect for medical purposes: Bark.

The preferred solvent is boiling water.

Effects: Diuretic, febrifuge, analgesic.

Native American Use:

* Salix bark has been found as being rich in salicin which is the primary chemical from which aspirin from. Natives as well as others from the past employed Salix bark for treating illnesses like rheumatism and colds as well as headaches. They made use of the properties of analgesia and febrifuge that this plant has.

The Salix bark extract proved effective in relieving pain for those suffering from tendinitis, bursitis and arthritis. The anti-inflammatory properties of the decoction helped decrease swelling as well as the discomfort that comes with these ailments.

ADVICE: Due to the high content of salicin, it may aggravate existing conditions including ulcers, diarrhea.

AVERAGE: The willow plant has a high concentration of cadmium that it gathers from the environment around it. Cadmium can be a poisonous metal to our body.

Tips for the Beginner GARDENER The roots of willow are widely spread throughout the area of the tree. This could lead to the death of adjacent trees.

Witch Hazel

Binomial Name: Hamamelis virginiana

It is spread out across forests and in woods all across all of the Eastern and Mid-Eastern parts of the United States, from the Atlantic shoreline up to the Mississippi River and the Great Lakes Region.

Specifications: This tree is able to grow at least 30 feet in height. The bark is unique in that it is brown on the outside and bright red on the interior. Numerous twisted trunks emerge from the rootstalk that is abundantly populated with alternate leaves that have serrated edges. On the underside of leaves, the blossoms emerge in clusters of 7 or more.

They have petals that are small, oval, twisty as well as yellow.

Parts that are to be collected to use for medical reasons Leaves and bark.

The preferred solvents are boiling water or alcohol.

Effects: Expectorant, diuretic, analgesic, antiseptic.

Native American Use:

* Native Americans used the tea of dried or fresh leaves for a cleanser to treat burns, eye injuries as well as for the treating hemorrhoids. The tea was also beneficial for the treatment of skin problems like athlete's feet (due due to its antifungal qualities) as well as eczema. In the event of drinking, it assisted in removing phlegm, and also acted as a strong febrifuge. It was also used for treating sore throats as well as an astringent for curing dysentery.

* The bark's inner layer is where the therapeutic properties have the greatest concentration, therefore teas, decoctions and other drinks made with it can be more potent.

* Native Americans used to harvest the buds of young plants in springtime for a drink, believed to be an effective tonic.

It is important to note that Twigs were often used to divinate rods. The water diviners chose the witch hazel branch with the form of an Y. They walked slowly an area in which they searched for water. The stick began to move, this indicated that at the area, there was water under.

Wormwood

Binomial Name: Arthemisia campestris

The location is widely distributed in dry areas across the North American Continent, both within Canada and in the United States and Canada.

Particulars: Arthemisia Campestris has a two-year existence. Its first year it appears as a rose that is deeply divided and almost straight, grayish green leaves. After the second season, the stems are reddish and grow out at the base. They are covered by smaller and deeper cut leaves. Stems are adorned with hairs, and they have tiny yellow flowers on top.

Parts that can be collected to use for medical reasons: leaves and flowers.

The most preferred solvent is dilute alcohol.

Effects: Vermifuge, febrifuge, sedative, carminative, emmenagogue.

Native American Use:

* The medical benefits of the Arthemisa Campestris are many and are well-known. The natives would take a bite to swallow and swallow the liquid from leaves in order to ease digestive gas and make usage of its anticonvulsant and carminative properties.

* The leaves decoction produced a strong sweat, drinks that reduced fever. The decoction also served as a remedy in eliminating intestinal worms, other parasites, and for improving blood flow in the instances of low menstrual flow.

* A bunch of herbs that were fresh was left to dry, and was then utilized for the smudging ceremony, for smudging the attendees.

* The herb's freshness was utilized in sweat lodge rituals.

Warning: Arthemisia can be toxic consumed in excess.

Warning: Do not take the product if you're already taking anticonvulsants.

Yarrow

Binomial Name: Achillea millefolium

Area: Spread throughout The North American continent in gardens and forest.

Specifications: This plant can be found all across North America. It produces a variety of stems out of a rhizome in the ground that may reach 3 feet high. Hairy bi-pinnate cauline leaves cover the stems and dimensions decrease as they reach the upper part in the plants. The dense clusters of 20 up to forty white blooms with five petals, and yellow stamens, are found on the upper part of the plant.

Parts to be collected for use in medical research: Leaves flowering, stems, and leaves.

Most preferred Solvents: Diluted Alcohol or water.

Effects: Astringent, diuretic, diaphoretic, analgesic.

Native American Use:

It is a little-known plant that has been widespread use by Native Americans, usage of this plant involves smoking of dried and pulverized leaves in order to treat chronic epistaxis and headaches.

The poultice made of leaves provides a potent anti-inflammatory impact in cases of mastitis or other common skin disorders like burnings, eczemas and injuries. The leaves are used to treat emergencies should you get injured when you are in the woodlands. Actually, when put directly on the area of injury the leaves can stop bleeding.

* Native Americans also used the tea derived from the fresh plant to increase sweating, as well as treat inflammations, fevers as well as illnesses. The decoction also functions as powerful diuretic and believed to be purifying. The decoction was also utilized for its analgesic properties to wash the body for insect bites.

* The infusion made from leaves alone has an effect of sedation and assists in sleep and relaxation and sleep. The decoction made that was made from only the roots was used to cleanse acne.

The yarrow tincture is efficient in decreasing excess menstrual blood flow (hypermenorrhea).

The yarrow-based salves are beneficial if they're rubbed into the chest of the patient in cases of bronchitis.

* The smudging action of the dried plant will keep mosquitoes from afar.

Warning: It contains Thujone, which is a carcinogen substance which is why it should be used to be used in moderation.

Chapter 13: Yellow Dock

Nominal Name of Binomial: Rumex crispus

The location is diffused across in the North American continent in gardens and in yards.

Specifications: This tiny perennial plant can be found across North America. It could grow to 40 inches at the taproot, which appears brown on the outside while being it is yellow interior. It can be sunk to 30 inches into the soil. The leaves at the base are long thin and narrow with curly edges. Flowers are set on high on the plant, in the form of white or red vertical racemes. The seeds can be harvested in the winter months at the highest point of the plant.

The parts to be collected for use in medical research such as Rhizome.

The most popular solvents are alcohol, water.

Effects: Astringent, tonic, laxative, anti-inflammatory.

Native American Use:

* The anti-inflammatory qualities of the plant were utilized to treat inflammation by Native Americans to treat swollen joints as well arthritis. The application of a poultice made of fresh, mashed the rhizome is recommended for these conditions.

* The juice extracted from the rhizome, or the roast seeds has amazing astringent qualities for treating dysentery and diarrhea.

* The powder produced by drying the rhizome was utilized for anti-hemorrhagic purposes on wounds.

* The decoction from the dried rhizome which has a bitter taste can be a potent liver stimulant and assists in detoxifying blood.

Warning: Avoid using in the case of kidney problems. The large amount of tannin in yellow dock may be harmful if eaten in large quantities.

Yew

Binomial Name: Taxus brevifolia

Where: The wild yew bushes are throughout The Pacific Coast States, from Northern California up to Graham Island and also in the North-Western region of Idaho.

Specifications: This evergreen tree grows at up to 60 feet size. Leaves are small and lanceolate in order to prevent heat loss throughout the cold winter months. The fruits are tiny, red berries that are in the form of a cup. They also have one black seed in its middle.

The parts to be collected to use for medical reasons such as leaves, fruits and barks.

Most preferred solvents: alcohol Water, alcohol.

Effects: Astringent, tonic, laxative.

Native American Use:

* Native Americans used the poultice made from fresh needles for an dressing for burns and wounds. burns. The needles were also used as decoctions to make an antiseptic and analgesic wash.

* The decoction of bark was utilized to treat stomach pain.

* The berries of yew were eaten in raw form to induce abortions, increase menstrual flow or trigger the contraction of the uterus during challenging births.

Warning: This plant is poisonous, therefore consume it with medical supervision. The plant can cause abortions.

Yucca

Binomial Name: Yucca filamentosa

The location is similar to that of the other succulent plants It is mostly scattered in the scorching dry deserts in Mexico and the Southern United States and Mexico.

Specifications: This desert plant doesn't have a root, and only rises up out of the ground as the form of a clump of basal lengthy, sword-shaped leaves. The basal leaves, we get one spike which can extend up to 60 inches. The spike is covered by a group of bell-shaped white blooms. The period of blooming during which the flowers can be enjoyed extends from the end of spring until the end of the summer.

Parts that can be collected to use for medical reasons: roots and leaves.

The most popular solvents are alcohol Water, alcohol.

Effects: Analgesic, antiemetic, purgative.

Native American Use:

* Native Americans used this plant to wash their bodies. It is rich in saponins. the yucca extract was used to make a soap from natural ingredients as well as to get rid of head lice.

* The root decoction that is dried is used to treat the symptoms of rheumatism, gout and gout. It is an effective laxative. The water filtered by the leaves' poultices helps to soothe vomiting that is not controlled.

Chapter 14: Zizia Aurea (Golden Alexander)

Binomial Name: Zizia aurea

The location: Golden Alexander is native to the Atlantic areas in the North American continent, but it has spread to areas of the Midwestern in both Canada as well as Canada and the United States. It is a fan of moist habitats.

The characteristics of this perennial flower is able to grow up at a maximum of three feet in height. The leaves are lance-shaped with sharp margins and split into three or two the lobes. Lower leaves are larger and are organized into groupings of 3. Lower leaves are smaller. They are situated on the upper leaves and are placed into umbrella-shaped clusters. Each flower measures smaller than half a centimeter long, and contains five sepals and five yellow petals and five stamens. The fruits are tiny, egg-shaped and are in green.

Parts that should be collected to use for medical reasons: Flowers leaves, roots and flowers.

The most popular solvents are alcohol and water.

Effects: Analgesic, febrifuge.

Native American Use:

* Native Americans used dried root powder to provide powerful pain relief for teas and decoctions. Tea made from leaves and flowers can be used to treat Menstrual Pain and Pre-Menstrual Syndrome.

Chapter 15: Equipment and Materials needed for making

A tool that is appropriate is the one that's right for the task. This is a crucial idea to be aware of in every making activity including woodworking, cooking and even baking.

If you are equipped with the proper equipment, you will work quicker and more efficiently. There is less risk of cut or wounds that are not intended and, even more importantly it is less damaging to the surroundings and plants when you make clean cuts or digging more deeply.

Below is an overview of the most important items you'll need to get started exploring the wild easily.

A Plant Identification Handbook

It is likely to be an important device you'll require. A clear identification of the plant can tell you if it's edible or poisonous when it is endangered, as well as the best parts to choose to use for food or medicinal purposes.

Clippers and a Sharp Knife

Clippers and scissors are useful instruments. They permit clean cuts, and reduce the damage for the plant. I would recommend that you make the investment and purchase good quality equipment because it will enable you to cut cleanly without much effort, and reduce the chance of accidentally cutting your own self (even in the case of harder plants and roots like Echinacea). They will ultimately help you do the job and will last for years.

A different useful tool is a well-cut knife which allows you to create an exact 45 degree cut in plants that clippers aren't able to do.

Gloves

Important tools to safeguard your hands from injury when dealing mit stinging, thorny plants or with knives.

Trowel and Folding Shovel

They're invaluable for digging up roots. A scoop is sufficient for the majority of roots.

However, when digging deeper roots one must carry an adjustable shovel. They are available in a variety of sizes and are priced accordingly. When folded, they are not big enough to take up too the area.

Saw

This is vital in the process of harvesting branches due to obvious reasons. This will create clean cuts within the tree's trunk. The tree is less susceptible to infection and disease.

Paper Bags and Clean Linen Sheets

While Native American traditions allow only clear sheets for storing plants after they have been picked from their location to the home Brown paper bags are a great alternative. Their primary purpose serve is to absorb water and aid in the transpiration of the herb. Bags made of plastic should avoid at all times as they promote mold growth.

Becoming an Experienced Wild Crafter

The only way to learn is through experience. the necessary tools to get how to navigate the plant life and your area, or pinpoint areas. Naturally, there are certain tips for speeding this process

Take your time when you are with your plants. Take a look at them with interest and make use of your nose and touches as well as eyes. It is possible to observe interesting things in even the most commonly used plant species, the way it alters between seasons and even from year to year in certain instances.

Note down: every time you spot a plant take note of where it is located as well as its neighbors and the insects you have found. You'll be able to identify the patterns quickly and know what plants you require quickly.

Maintain a sketchbook, Even if you're no Leonardo Da Vinci and barely understand what a pencil actually is I suggest you keep a notebook of species you can identify. It can help you develop an habitude of engaging in attentive and detailed observation of the species.

Create your own herbarium by keeping plants, leaves and buds inside the middle of your book, for a while until it's dry. After that, you can put it in the notebook.

Photography: Technology today allows this to be done more easily as compared to when I began crafting wild. You are able to easily snap pictures with your mobile and then write notes on the image.

Safe Wildcrafting Rules

Make sure you follow these basic rules while you are wildcrafting. This will help you are able to get wet with the utmost safety within this amazing world. With time, you'll gain confidence and become familiar with the environment around you and be aware of what to choose and leave.

Find out the species of plant prior to harvesting. There are many poisonous plants that look exactly like the ones used in medical treatment.

If you are unsure don't harvest. Make a photo and verify from home, or talk to the neighborhood Extension Office.

Don't "taste test" plants you aren't familiar with.

Make sure you are aware of species that are endangered in the area around you.

Reach the 10percent rule Only harvest 10percent or less of what you discover so as to ensure that you do not harming the ecosystem.

Do not harvest near areas of urbanization for example, roadsides, high-tension trellis or railway tracks.

Beware: You could be intolerant or allergic to one plant, and you're not even aware of. If you are trying a new plant, make sure you use small quantities and test only one new thing at one moment.

Be aware Keep your eyes open: although wildcrafting could appear as if it's hiking, it's quite different. There are many dangers hidden while exploring the forest like the stinging of plants, thorns or even holes in the ground which could result in ankle sprains.

Beware of plants with sap that is white This is a huge signal that this plant can be toxic.

Umbel flowers: be aware of this. A lot of curative plants like the yarrow flower in umbels, however there are many toxic looks that look similar. Make sure you know the plant you're picking.

Take extra care when handling mushrooms, as they may contain poisonous substances.

A lot of herbs resemble mint but aren't smelt or taste minty. A lot of novice wildcrafters have gotten caught out by taking poisonous looks-alikes of mint.

If you spot animals eating certain herb, that isn't an indication that the herb is consumed.

Animals have developed tolerance to certain toxic plant species.

Free Apps for Plant Recognition

Technology today makes my work easier than ever before I started. There are a lot of sites and applications on the web which can help you find the different plants you'll meet.

Below are my most-loved apps for free:

*"Like" That Garden: You can upload your photo and provide your immediate recognition to the plant. The recognition isn't always 100 percent reliable. It is best when you have flowers, so make your own judgement.

* Leafsnap: This program allows you to take a leaf photo to give you instant confirmation of the species. The photo must be taken against a white backdrop, that is not always practical.

* ID Weeds: Developed by the University of Missouri. It recognizes the plant upon input of certain characteristics. It is less practical as

the other two, however more trustworthy. Also, you can check their picture database.

* Vtree: Created at Virginia Tech, it gives the list of plant species that are in the area by taking your GPS coordinates. It also offers plant images as well as description.

"About Herbs" is a database of herbal remedies and plants that includes pictures as well as descriptions and medicinal preparations. I would suggest using it with any of the other applications mentioned above.

Suggested Gathering Times

Above ground or aerial constituents in the range of 6. a.m.-10 a.m. in the morning just before they begin to wilt in the sunlight. Certain varieties are best when you harvest leaves prior to blooming. The ability to observe the bud's hue when you select the most popular flowers once they have begun to flower. The most common lunar cycle to collect aerial elements is either before or following when the moon is full.

Roots: Early in the morning, before sunrise. pick after seeding should it be necessary.

Biennials harvest during the autumn of the first year, or in the season of the following year. Traditional times are a New Moon.

Barks: Harvest in the fall or spring. Do not necessarily cut. Pick a complete plant. Thinner trees are appropriate for city areas that are dense, but most healthy trees will not quit. If you are only taking the small leaves, you must ensure that you do not make your tree more vulnerable to fungal decay. To prevent pollarding, the inside cambium (or bark) is the most interconnected bark of all, with smaller stumps and small trees to copping. The cambium will continue to produce. The three-quarters of the light that is waning is the old bark method.

Pitches and Saps Pick them up in winter or in the early spring.

Produce and fruits: Harvest but with some minor differences once mature. For example, bananas, ripe pods of beans in scarlet, etc.

Drying Out

Avoid washing the bulb or trees. For cleaning off rodents and dust shake the bulbs. If the quantities are suitable put bundles on the stem's base, having sizes that are 1 1/4 inches and less. When they are placed on walls, they could even be scattered in a loose manner for drying.

Barks: Cut the outer bark, if required. It is also known as"flipping.

Roots: Spread them out or make a circle. Rinsing is not always able to eliminate soil particles. Pressure hoses are sometimes required, along with brushing with a hand, especially when using clay. Slice lengthwise to get lengthy, heavy roots with no aromatic qualities.

When both plant components are fragile, remain dry. The lower portion of the plant should squeeze the trees that hang. Cut a large plant root into two pieces to determine if your heart is not dry.

Storage

Beware of heat that is too light or excessive, and could cause the destruction of aromatic compounds as well as other essential ingredients. Food-grade plastic bags, fiber barrels and other containers that release moisture and oxygen will ensure the consistency and strength throughout the time they're hot.

Mark the date and place.

Crushed or broken herbs are less valuable often than fresh herbs and are completely.

Herbal Preparations

Infusions are made by submerging an herb into either hot or cold (not hot) water. The water, which is not drinking water, may be one of the purest sources you can come across. It's better to offer drinking water that is derived from rainwater, excellent streams or wells, as well as bottle water. The herbs that contain powerful volatile oils should be to be infused into cold water (those which have an distinctive smell like essential oils or fragrance). If you use warm water, certain herbs are effective.

Based on the type of plant, it is possible to leave them for a period of 15 minutes up to a night, in order to take in the essential elements of the plant. To make infusions and decoctions, earthenware or glass vessels are excellent. Because they aren't damaged by the heat, pint or quart canning jars work well as well as the screw cap keeps the nutrients from floating inside the steam.

Chapter 16: Recipes for Teas and Decoctions

Herbal Tea Recipe

Herbal teas are different from one another and generally brewed teas since they don't come from the same source. They're the blends of plants, flowers and dried fruits that are prepared similarly to tea. Herbal teas do not contain caffeine and are often able to lower blood pressure, are tasty flavors and can improve digestion. Also, most of them have no calories, and they are free of sugar.

Raspberry Tea

Serving size: 1 serving

Time to brew: 10 mins

Ingredients:

* 1 C. water

* 1/4 1 c. dried raspberries leaves

* 1/4 C. dried lemongrass

* 1/2 1. dried flowers of chamomile

1/2 C. dry orange peel

Directions:

1. Mix together all dried herbs mentioned above.

2. Boil water to boil.

3. Mix 1 teaspoon of tea blend to a cup.

4. Pour boiling water on it. Close the lid and allow it to let it sit for 5 to 10 minutes. The longer it takes it is, the more tannin gets taken out.

5. Drink hot or cold drinks or even iced.

The nutritional information per serving

* Calories: 40

* Carbs: 12 g

* Fat: 0 g

* Protein: 0 g

* Sodium: 2 mg

* Sugar: 0 g

Hibiscus-Ginger Tea

Serving size: prepare 4 cups

Time to brew: 15 minutes

Ingredients:

* 4 * 4. water

* 1 tbsp. Leaves of hibiscus

* 1 tbsp. grated fresh ginger

* 3-5 mint leaves

Directions:

1. In a pot, boil water.

2. Combine hibiscus with ginger, then mix in a separate container.

3. Pour boiling water over the tea Cover, then let it steep for 10 to 12 minutes.

4. The tea's color is likely to change from a ruby red color, after which you can add mint leaves for refreshing flavor.

5. Serve chilled or hot.

Information on nutrition per serving

* Calories: 1

* Carbs: 1 g

* Fat: 0 g

* Protein: 0 g

* Sodium: 1 mg

* Sugar: 0 g

Mint Tea

Serving size: two portions

Time to brew: 8. mins

Ingredients:

* 2 1. water

* 15-20 fresh mint leaves

* 2 slices of lemon

* 1 tsp. honey (optional)

Directions:

1. In a teapot, heat the water.

2. Take the pot off the stove and add of the leaves. Then cover the pot, and let it sit for five minutes. Add more time to enjoy an intense mint flavor.

3. Place the contents in a glass or glass.

4. Sprinkle honey on top and decorate with lemon slices.

5. Drink hot or cold.

The nutritional information per serving

* Calories: 150

* Carbs: 26 g

* Fat: 5 g

* Protein: 3 g

* Sodium: 75 mg

* Sugar: 15 g

Sweet and Spicy Herb Tea

Serving size: Make 1 serving

The time to drink: 10 mins

Ingredients:

* 1 C. water

* 1/2 tbsp. cloves

* 1 tbsp. dried stevia

* 1/4 1. cinnamon stick

* 1/4 c. dried orange zest

* 1/4 1 c. dried flowers from chamomile

* 1/2 c. dried lemon verbena

Directions:

1. Blend the mixture and then use 1 teaspoon of tea mix.

2. The water should be boiling before pouring it over the tea blend.

3. Then cover the pot, and let it sit for five minutes or longer.

4. Pour into a glass to serve warm. Alternately, pour the drink into a glass with ice and serve it cold.

5. Take pleasure in the spicy and sweet flavor.

The nutritional information per serving

* Calories: 110

* Carbs: 31 g

* Fat: 3 g

* Protein: 2 g

* Sodium: 16 mg

* Sugar: 1 g

Basil Tea

Serving size: 1 serving

Time to brew: 5 minutes

Ingredients:

* 1 C. water

* 1 tsp. basil leaves

* 1/4 tsp. dried ginger

* 1/2 tsp. cinnamon powder

* 1 tsp. honey (optional)

Directions:

1. Bring the water to a boil and then include the basil leaves, ginger and cinnamon.

2. Allow it to stand for five minutes.

3. Then strain and add honey for a better taste.

4. Place the contents in a cup, then serve hot.

The nutritional information per serving

* Calories: 10

* Carbs: 3 g

* Fat: 0 g

* Protein: 0 g

* Sodium: 1 mg

* Sugar: 0 g

Decoctions

They are also other types of natural remedies. It is the process of extracting therapeutic properties of the herb through the process of slowing the herb in water until it changes colour, scent and savoury characteristics. Decoctions are prepared by the method, which allows herbaceous or plant substances to expel their active components while the boiling process. This way, the different chemical compounds found in the plant can be removed by mixing them in warm water. Decoctions are the most widely-used sources of herbalism-based medicine. The bark or roots of plants are rich in medicinal qualities however, it can be difficult to extract these tough parts of plants like bark of willow. Decoctions can be used to remove tannins that can be bitter and harsh, and aid in easing to ease indigestion.

Decoctions were used for the treatment of a myriad of ailments throughout history and are particularly used in herbal medicines. It is effective in the treatment of various ailments, like the purification of blood, liniments that treat issues with the skin such as acne and dermatitis as well as fornics in the treatment of dryness, as well as inflammations like eczema and psoriasis.

In general, they're believed as being beneficial in the treatment of muscle and joint problems like arthritis, rheumatism, cramps and so on.

Making Herb-Infused Decoctions

Herbs can be utilized for making herbal decoctions but they also can be utilized to make infusions. This involves making herbal infusions by boiling the leaves with water over a longer period in comparison to the time required to prepare decoctions. This way the active ingredients will become more efficient as they will be concentrated inside the water, not just within the leaves themselves. Decoctions are created by heating herbs and water to the point that the water reveals its colour, scent and flavor characteristics. This way, the various organic chemical compounds found in the plant are easily removed by mixing them in warm water. Decoctions are commonly used as sources of herbalism herbal remedies. But, they may also make from bark, roots, and they are not as rich in beneficial properties as extracts made from plants, leaves seeds, leaves, etc.

Below is a listing of drinks you could explore:

Basil Decoction

Method:

1. Cook 2-3 tablespoons of basil leaves in one cup of water.

2. Cover the pot with a lid and let it steep for about 10 minutes.

3. If you wish the blend to be concentrated You can boost the quantity of basil leaves are used in the preparation of your drink.

4. Then, take the hot mixture and strain it through an strainer or cheesecloth to a cup that is empty.

5. Clean the filter thoroughly If it has been used prior to storing the filter for use later on.

6. Take this herbal hot tea two times a day for the best outcomes.

Other ingredients you might consider adding to the mix are rosemary, mint leaves or lavender.

It is also worth noting that rosemary could be utilized as an alternative to basil for an even stronger mix.

German Chamomile Decoction

Method:

1. Cook a couple of tablespoons of flowers from chamomile in a glass of water.

2. Cover the pot with a lid, and allow to steep for 10 minutes.

3. Make your chamomile tea and strain it with a cheesecloth or strainer into an empty glass.

4. Clean the filter thoroughly when it is used, and then store it to use in the future.

5. Consume this hot herbal tea at least twice a day to get the most outcomes.

It is possible to add additional ingredients to your recipe for example, rosemary, mint leaves or lavender.

Additionally, take note of the fact that rosemary could be utilized as an alternative to chamomile in order to create an even stronger blend.

Chicory Decoction

Method:

1. Cook 1-2 tablespoons of chicory root in a Cup of water.

2. Then cover with a lid, and allow to steep for 5-10 minutes.

3. Then, take the hot mixture and strain it with the strainer or cheesecloth in an empty container.

4. Make sure to thoroughly clean the filter when it is used, and then store the filter for use later on.

5. Consume this hot herbal tea two times a day for the best outcomes.

It is possible to add additional ingredients to your recipe for example, rosemary, mint leaves or lavender.

The chicory plant can be utilized instead of chamomile to make a more potent blend.

Ginger Decoction

Method:

1. Make a boil of 1-2 tablespoons ginger in a glass of water.

2. Close the lid, cover and let it steep for about 10 minutes.

3. Make sure you take your hot concoction and strain it through an strainer or cheesecloth to an empty container.

4. Clean the filter thoroughly when it is used, and then store the filter for use later on.

5. Consume this hot herbal tea at least twice a day to get the most outcomes.

Other ingredients you might be considering adding to the mix are rosemary, mint leaves and lavender.

Ginkgo Berry Decoction

Method:

1. Make a boil of 1-2 tablespoons Ginkgo in one cup of water.

2. Close the lid, cover and let it steep for about 10 minutes.

3. Make sure you take your hot concoction and strain it through an strainer or cheesecloth to an empty container.

4. Clean the filter thoroughly If it has been used prior to storing the filter for use later on.

5. Take this herbal hot tea two times a day for the best results.

There is a possibility of adding some other ingredients into your drink for example, rosemary, mint leaves or lavender.

Ginseng Decoction

Method:

1. Infuse 2 tablespoons of ginseng into the water in a cup.

2. Cover the pot with a lid and let it steep for about 10 minutes.

3. Make sure you take your hot concoction and strain it with an strainer or cheesecloth to an empty glass.

www.ingramcontent.com/pod-product-compliance
Lightning Source LLC
Chambersburg PA
CBHW051727020426
42333CB00014B/1187